together OR separate
knitting the new twinset

Ann McCauley

Martingale®
& COMPANY

Together or Separate:
Knitting the New Twinset

© 2008 by Ann McCauley

Martingale®
& C O M P A N Y

Martingale & Company®
20205 144th Ave. NE
Woodinville, WA 98072-8478 USA
www.martingale-pub.com

Printed in China
13 12 11 10 09 08   8 7 6 5 4 3 2 1

**Library of Congress Cataloging-in-
Publication Data**

Library of Congress Control Number:
2008025396

ISBN: 978-1-56477-860-4

CREDITS

President & CEO Tom Wierzbicki
Publisher Jane Hamada
Editorial Director Mary V. Green
Managing Editor Tina Cook
Technical Editor Ursula Reikes
Copy Editor Durby Peterson
Design Director Stan Green
Production Manager Regina Girard
Illustrator Adrienne Smitke
Cover & Text Designer Shelly Garrison
Photographer Brent Kane

MISSION STATEMENT

Dedicated to providing quality products
and service to inspire creativity.

dedication

I would like to dedicate this book to our hands and their innate creativity.

acknowledgments

The intense discipline and focus required to accomplish a book project would not be possible without the love and support of my life partner, Tom. I am eternally grateful to my mother, Becky, who not only taught me to knit but also allowed me the freedom to be who I am, even when her choices for me might have been different than my own.

No book is a solitary effort. Everyone at Martingale & Company deserves the greatest praise, especially Ursula Reikes for her amazing level of patience.

Thanks to Dave Van Stralen at Louet Sales and Peggy Wells at Brown Sheep Company for providing yarn.

Huge gratitude to all the wonderful knitters I've met for their encouragement. I'd love to list each and every one of you, if space permitted! I appreciate all the amazing yarn shop owners I have met for how very much they do and what they provide for knitters. Getting to know the members of different knitting guilds has also been a great joy.

CONTENTS

Introduction 9

Alphabet of Musings 10

Together or Separate Designs

Striped Stockinette
T-Shirt and Cowl
17

Mock Pleat and
Rib Turtleneck and Skirt
21

Eyelet and Ruffle
Cardigan and Shell
27

Moss and Feather Faggot
Cardigan and Shell
33

Seed and Triple Gull Cable
Cardigan and Skirt
39

Uneven Cable Turtleneck,
Headband, and Vest
47

Twisted Rib and Cable Dress
or Pullover and Wristlets
55

Arrowhead Lace
Cardigan and Shell
61

Chain and Double Cable
Cardigan and Socks
67

INTRODUCTION

As I continue to knit, lovingly and obsessively, it seems only logical that I would be led in the direction of the twinset. If one knit garment is heavenly to wear, then two must certainly be twice as wonderful! The twinset is now my favorite thing to design. My first twinset creation was the traditional cardigan and shell, although my mind was already racing ahead to the possibilities in broadening this interpretation. This could mean my new favorite thing to knit included everything. How very convenient!

It occurred to me that I wanted these symbiotic twins to be updated and refined. I could envision them as wanting to be independent as well as interdependent, but never codependent. After all, knitting is a metaphor for life for so many of us.

There was even a correlation between the twinset and my parents' interesting generation, since Hollywood in its glamorous era of the 1940s helped make the twinset a star. By the 1950s, the twinset was walking the halls of colleges and high schools as well.

Being a member of the baby boom generation, as are all of us who were born between 1946 and 1964, and in view of my generation's love of redefining, I determined that the twinset in its new manifestation was ready to have a new name. Who better to query than one's own life partner as to what might be a more appropriate name for this coming manifestation of a classic? Hence, the term *together or separate* became his insightful gift to me.

Last and far from least, what could offer more versatility and flexibility for our contemporary lifestyle and wardrobe than a together-or-separate approach to knitting. Please enjoy the knitting and the wearing of what is offered here.

For many of us, knitting encourages musing. It creates the opportunity to ruminate, reflect, intently consider, ponder, contemplate, or simply explore a source of inspiration. I offer this eclectic alphabet of musings, which includes practical knitting tips, suggestions about physical awareness for knitters, and hopefully, thought-provoking concepts about our beloved and shared art of knitting.

ATTENTIVENESS

Knitting offers us lessons in paying attention. It helps us to be in the present. This could be among the many reasons we love knitting so much. When we are in the present, there exists the possibility of having more fun and increased energy. As one becomes a more experienced knitter, it may feel that the amount of attention we need to give to our knitting is lessened. Quite possibly, it is more accurate to say that the type of attention that we give to our knitting shifts from being solely a mental focus to include a visceral or sensory focus. Cultivate this awareness. Many knitters I meet share that they can simply feel when they have made a mistake.

BREATH AND KNITTING

Once we've settled into a few rows, knitting provides an excellent opportunity to observe the breath. Naturally, the breath may become quieter as we knit, since we are not being highly physically active. Observe the exhalation. Observe what qualities it possesses. When we exhale, it is our opportunity to let go, to empty out, to release. When

we let go of something old, we make room for something new. When we are born, the first thing that happens with the breath is that we exhale. Observe the inhalation. When we inhale we receive. We renew, regenerate, replenish, restore, recharge.

Since we are often counting when we knit, there is an opportunity to count our breaths as well. How many counts or stitches does our inhalation and exhalation utilize? Again, this is something that we are simply observing without the need to judge or compare. A specific counted-breathing exercise can easily be done while knitting and can be coordinated with any counting of stitch patterns we might be doing.

What numbers you utilize in a counted-breathing exercise may well depend on how quickly or slowly you knit. By all means, choose a number that you are comfortable with. For the purpose of an example, let's say I knit four stitches in about five or six seconds. Inhale for the count of four, hold the inhalation for the count of four, and then exhale for the same amount of time. Repeat this counted breathing 10 times with all inhalations and exhalations occurring through the nose. If 10 times feels like too many, there are no hard-and-fast rules here. Do what feels right to you.

Another interesting breathing exercise that works easily with knitting is to stick out your tongue and roll it inward into the shape of a drinking straw. Apparently rolling the tongue in this manner is a genetic ability and this exercise will not be an option if you are unable to do

so. If this does work for you, inhale through the tongue. This will produce a long, slow and sustained inhalation. Then, exhale through the nose. You may notice that your exhalation feels longer or more thorough, your head feels clearer, or that your energy feels better. You may even feel slightly light-headed if you have been breathing shallowly prior to trying this. You may notice any number of things and remember that you are simply observing.

If there is an area in your body that begins to feel tension or tightness while you are knitting, you might want to explore breathing directly into that area to achieve more openness and movement there.

BUTTONHOLES

If you are in search of the preferred knitted buttonhole, I would nominate the one-row horizontal buttonhole as your candidate. It is the buttonhole with the cleanest appearance, and it requires no further finishing or reinforcing once it is worked. It can be worked from either the right side or wrong side of your work. I advise working the button-band side first. If you position and mark where the buttons will be sewn, you will have a clear guide as to where the buttonholes will be placed. First and last buttons should generally be no farther than ½" from the edge of the garment. Exceptions would be design choices. It is also a good idea to purchase one extra button in case a button breaks. I mention this because I am fond of mother-of-pearl buttons on sweaters. They come in many colors, are understated, and don't compete with the textured sweaters I love to knit. Sometimes these shell buttons can vary in thickness, and a very thin one may break over time. If the selection is good, you can sort through them for ones that feel strong.

Buttons on a woman's sweater are traditionally sewn on the left side. They may be sewn with matching-colored thread or with a split strand of matching yarn. Buttoned buttons on knit garments often lie best when sewn with a shank. To make the shank, leave a space of approximately ⅛" to ¼" between the sweater and the button. The amount of space left will form the shank and will depend on the weight or bulk of the garment; a finer knit requires less space and a heavier one requires more. After you have sewn through the holes of the button three or four times, bring the needle and yarn through to the right side, underneath the button, and wrap the yarn or thread around itself in the ⅛" to ¼" space several times. Finish by passing the yarn and needle through to the wrong side and fasten off.

working the one-row horizontal buttonhole

1. Work to the buttonhole and with yarn in front, slip a stitch purlwise. Place and leave yarn in back. *Slip the next stitch from the left needle and pass the first slipped stitch over it; repeat from * the number of times that creates the appropriate-sized hole for the button you have chosen. The buttonhole for a flat button will be smaller than for a raised button of the same diameter. Slip the last bound-off stitch to the left needle and turn your work.

2. With the yarn at the back of your work, cable cast on one stitch more than you bound off and turn your work.

3. With the yarn in back, slip the first stitch from the left needle and pass the extra cast-on stitch over it to close the buttonhole.

I utilized the one-row horizontal buttonhole in the Seed and Triple Gull Cable Cardigan. It appears to be a vertical buttonhole on the sweater, but it is worked horizontally since the seed stitch is picked up and worked from the front edge outward.

There is also a place for the vertical buttonhole. It is a bit more labor intensive with a few more ends to weave in when finished, but is most effective in ribs that are worked from the cardigan front edge outward. In the Chain and Double Cable Cardigan, with its K2, P2 ribbing, you will definitely find that the vertical buttonhole lies best when worked between two purl stitches. In this sweater the vertical buttonhole appears to be worked horizontally because the ribbing is picked up along the outer edge and worked outward. As with the horizontal buttonhole above, you will want to position and mark the buttons first.

working the vertical buttonhole

1. Work to the edge of the button-hole. Turn the work and knit back and forth in rows to the desired depth of the buttonhole. Cut the yarn, leaving a 6" to 10" tail for future use.

2. Attach the yarn to the first stitch at the base of the tail. Knit back and forth across the next section

of stitches (from the end of the first buttonhole to the beginning of the second buttonhole) until this section is as deep as the first. Repeat this process until all buttonholes are worked.

3. On the next full row, you will close all buttonholes by working across all stitches. If you pick up the cut strand from the button-hole edge along with your feed yarn and use both strands for two stitches, you will create a more secure edge at the outer edge of the buttonhole.

working the buttonhole stitch

Some buttonholes, such as the vertical buttonhole, require a bit of finishing or reinforcing to appear and function at their best. The buttonhole stitch provides this reinforcement.

Thread your tapestry needle using either a whole or split strand of yarn, depending on the weight of your yarn. Work from right to left around the buttonhole, with the needle pointing toward the center as illustrated. To avoid distorting the buttonhole, take care not to work your stitches too closely or tautly. This provides a cleaner, more secure inner edge.

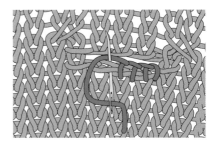

Buttonhole-stitch edge

CHANGING COLORS FOR HORIZONTAL STRIPES

The easiest type of color knitting may well be horizontal stripes. You can carry the yarn you are not using along the side of your work, and it will always be where you need it when you are working stripes that result in an even number of rows. It is as simple as bringing the new color strand under the old color strand and knitting with the new color. Just as in knitting with one color, be aware of tension and do not pull the yarn too tightly or loosely when you carry the color along the side.

DESIGN

Every time you follow a knitting pattern, you are going to design school. You are in the process of increasing your understanding of the elements of the pattern and acquiring new skills.

EYES

We use our eyes a lot when we knit—especially when we are just learning, working a more complex pattern, or knitting with black or dark-colored yarns. Granted, there are knitters whose level of expertise allows them to do so without requiring more than an occasional glance at their work. If your eyes feel strained, fatigued, or overworked, briskly rub the palms of your hands together until you feel that the friction is generating heat. Follow this by gently shaking your hands as if you were shaking off drops of water. Then, using a cupped hand position, bring your palms to rest over your eyes. Allow the entire area around the eyes to soften as your palms rest over your eyes. Allow the energy of your hands to renew the eye area. When you remove your hands from your eyes, explore the possibility of allowing a softer focus.

FLOOR

I don't feel I can encourage you enough to spend some time on the floor. Your body will thank you. When we are on the floor, our bodies will naturally lengthen out or start to stretch. I rarely, if ever, observe this happening from a seated position. Lying on the floor with both knees bent and the soles of your feet on the floor—with your feet (all ten toes directed forward), ankles, knees, and the interior of your hip sockets aligned—is especially beneficial to the spine. Your body may naturally start to explore tilting the pelvis, rolling up and down the spine one vertebra at a time, rolling from side to side, or hugging one knee at a time or both knees to the chest. These simple movements have a profound effect on the spine.

Floor position

GRAVITY

The force that holds us to the earth also influences our knitting. Notice how much all the yarn you purchase for a sweater weighs when it is in a bag. This will be the weight of your garment. That is why I love seams. They add increased structural integrity or internal support for the weight of the finished garment.

HOLDING

Inevitably, we hold some of the tension or stress we experience in our lives in our bodies. Often activities that involve repetitive motion will point these areas out to us. In our active daily lives, we may be too busy to be aware of where we might be holding tension. Contemplate the possibility of allowing the surface area of your body to be free of any tension. Visualize that there is a sense of strength at the core and a sense of ease at the surface. Allow the inner core to be what supports you, and allow that support to be generated from the inside and carried to the outer layer.

INTUITION

Intuition is accessible when we stay in the present. Staying in the present helps us to honor our first thought or first impulse. I find this helpful relative to knitting whether I'm shopping for yarn or starting a new design. I also find that intuition is easier to access when I become very quiet and still. Intuition leads us to a wellspring of creativity and carries us through the creative process.

JOINING TEXTURED SHOULDERS

In working shoulder seams that involve cable patterns or right and left twists, I find it helpful to seam through one strand of a stitch at a time (instead of two strands) for only these stitches, particularly at the beginning and end of cables and twists. This results in the cleanest matching of seamed stitches.

KINESTHESIA

Kinesthesia is the sense that detects bodily position, weight, or movement of the muscles, tendons, and joints. Knitting provides the possibility of observing subtle intrinsic movement in the body.

LESSONS

Consider the possibility that a mistake in your knitting is simply a lesson and an error that you will not have to make again.

MAKE ONE INCREASES

This increase is practically invisible. It is made by picking up the horizontal bar between two stitches and working into the front or back of the picked-up bar. Make one increases can be worked either knitwise or purlwise as is appropriate for the side you're working.

At the beginning of a row or for an increase slanting to the right, pick up the horizontal bar from back to front with the left needle and work the stitch through the front loop. The abbreviation *BFF* helps me remember this—pick up the bar from back to front and work the stitch through the front loop of the picked-up bar.

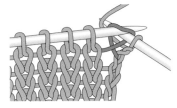

M1 at beg of row.

At the end of a row or for an increase slanting to the left, pick up the horizontal bar from front to back with the left needle and work through the back loop of the stitch. To remember this, think *FBB*—pick up the bar from front to back and work the stitch through the back loop of the picked-up bar. *BFF* comes before *FBB* alphabetically, and *BFF* comes at the beginning of a row.

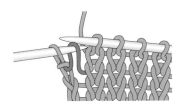

M1 at end of row.

NECKLINES

Each side of the sweater neck may be either worked separately by putting the rest of the stitches on a holder or worked at the same time by using separate balls of yarn. Working both sides at the same time helps you keep track of the stitches decreased on each side of the neck. For me, keeping track of the shaping for both sides at the same time simplifies and expedites the neck shaping. Working both sides at once requires attaching a second ball of yarn. Many instructions suggest that knitters do this on the first row of neck shaping after one side of the neck has been worked and before the initial decrease for the neckline. I prefer to work the entire first row with the original ball of yarn. Then on the second row, I attach the second ball of yarn to the second half of the neckline, which is usually when the second neck shaping is being worked.

(I say *usually* because there could be an exception, like a crewneck with a placket.)

Because I like to shape curves in sweaters by decreasing the first stitch and then utilizing the bind off, I attach the second ball of yarn to the second stitch for a smoother transition than would be achieved by attaching it to the first stitch. If your neckline is one of the exceptions to the rule of shaping at the neck edge on the second row, such as a crewneck with a placket as mentioned, then you would attach the second ball of yarn to the *first* stitch.

OPENNESS

Just as this is a key to what we experience in our lifetimes, I perceive that openness is a quality that greatly influences the design process. Unlike many designers, I allow my process to occur on the needles rather than in a sketch and a swatch. This approach allows the work to inform me, to show me where it wants to go or what it wants to become, and I am open to design directions I don't believe I would have seen otherwise.

PRESSING

This is the category in which knitters can take a lesson from seamstresses as to how to enhance their finished products. I'm not asking you to actually iron your finished knitted garments. However, here are some instances when a bit of steam as a light press can make a lovely difference. I steam through a linen tea towel or a cotton pressing cloth to protect the knitted fabric.

When joining stockinette or reverse stockinette side seams or underarm seams, you will see that the knitted fabric wants to roll inward toward the wrong side at the seam. With the garment inside out, pin the seam allowances on each edge of the actual seam so they are pushed to the outside, and then lightly steam.

If you have worked a three-needle bind off too tightly on a cotton sweater, such as the Eyelet and Ruffle Cardigan, you will notice that the cardigan's lower edges do not lie evenly with the fronts. Stretch, pin, and steam. This would not be a solution if working in wool, because wool has memory.

QUICK

Quick knits are wonderful, especially when knitting for gifts. What could be better than knitting a quick gift bag in a larger gauge, perhaps even adding a little I-cord closure, to put a bottle of wine in for taking to a dinner party. This has motivated more people to take up knitting than I could ever have imagined.

RIBBON

Ribbon was popular in the 1960s as a way to finish interior or exterior cardigan edges, particularly grosgrain ribbon for buttonhole and button bands as well as necklines. It served a wonderful, functional purpose then and still does today. Ribbons and trims are yet another way to enhance our knitted garments. Note that not all grosgrain ribbons are created equal. If you have access to

a shop specializing in ribbons and trims, you may find a better-quality grosgrain ribbon. The purpose of this ribbon is to face the inside of a collar or buttonhole band. A better-quality grosgrain usually has more body and is not as flimsy as a lower-quality grosgrain. Thus, the ribbon better serves the purpose of supporting a collar or buttonhole band and results in a more finished and professional look by covering the inner ridge of a stitch pick up.

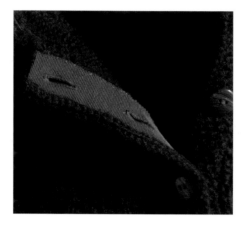

SPHERES

Visualize that you can physically sense and locate a spherical area in the innermost space of your pelvis. Once you have located or sensed that, give yourself a second sphere that is directly above the first and a long distance from it, located deep in the center of your chest. Be aware of the relationship between these two areas. Notice the difference in the way you feel when the second sphere is directly over the first, as opposed to behind it or in front of it. This simple image helps us balance the rib cage over the pelvis.

Give yourself a third sphere, directly above and a long distance from both the first and second, located deep in the center of the head or skull. Know that at any moment, whether you are knitting or moving through your day, you can observe where your three spheres are and shift them to an optimal, aligned relationship, which will create a greater sense of internal space, ease, and well-being. If you wish to explore this further, your three spheres might be narrowed down to points. You could also give yourself a sphere or point for each chakra, or energy center, in the body. A sphere or point outside of the body and above the head is helpful to sense and consider as well.

TENNIS BALLS

Doesn't this seem like an odd category for knitters? Read on; tennis balls are a great tool for self-care. Sitting in your favorite knitting spot, it's easy to place two tennis balls under your feet and gently roll the soles of the feet. Your feet will thank you! Tennis balls can also be utilized on the back by placing them between your back and the wall and then using the weight of your body to simply lean into them. Avoid placing them directly on the bones, vertebrae, or kidneys. Best results will come from placing them on either side of the spine, in the softer tissue, particularly between the shoulder blades and the spine. You control the amount of pressure by how much weight you use to lean into them. Bending and straightening the knees to roll the tennis balls vertically is helpful, as is just a small movement of your back from side to side to roll the tennis balls horizontally.

UNDERSTANDING

I always recommend to newer knitters that they not attempt to read through an entire knitting pattern before beginning to knit it. It can be too daunting, because it won't actually make sense to you until you're doing it step by step. Rather than becoming overwhelmed and doubting your ability to accomplish the pattern by reading all of it, read only the section that you're working on the needles, for example, the back, front, or sleeves.

VARIATIONS

This is just what knitters do. Honestly, I hardly know a knitter who can knit a pattern without changing something about it. It is my belief that this enriches what we knit and furthers how unique a knitted garment is. I couldn't even reknit the Twisted Rib and Cable Dress in its sweater variation without varying one of the pattern stitches.

WRIST STRETCH

My favorite wrist stretch follows. With the palm of one hand facing you, place the palm of the opposite hand against the back of that hand. Place the bottom-hand thumb against the little-finger edge of the top hand, and place the bottom-hand fingers against the thumb edge of the top hand. Lace the bottom-hand index finger between the index finger and the thumb of the top hand. Wrap the other three fingers around the base of the top-hand thumb. Keeping the top wrist and hand in line with the lower arm, use the bottom hand to gently rotate the top hand outward so that the little finger of the top hand moves to face you, and the thumb of the top hand faces away from you.

X STRETCH

Lie on the floor. Extend your arms and legs into an X position. Reach as far as you can to extend your X and make your body as long as possible. You can imagine that some kind and gentle person is pulling each finger and toe for you as you stretch. Extend, elongate, and open up space in your being.

YARN

Yarn is something that knitters never seem to have too much of! For the designs in this book, I've made every effort to utilize yarn that is readily available, good quality, and affordable.

ZEAL

This word accurately describes our enthusiastic devotion to knitting as well as our tireless diligence in its furtherance.

striped stockinette
T-SHIRT and COWL

A perpetual favorite, the crewneck long-sleeved T-shirt is knit in stripes and could also easily be knit in a solid color from this pattern. The possibilities of color combinations for the stripes are unlimited. As the weather cools, the cowl gives you a whole different look and is also fun to wear over a white T-shirt, with a jean jacket, or as you choose.

Skill Level: Easy ◧■□□

Size: Small (Medium, Large, Extra Large)

Finished Measurements

Bust: 36 (40, 44, 48)"

Length: 21¾ (22¾, 23¾, 24¾)"

Cowl circumference: 21"

Cowl length: 7"

MATERIALS

Cotton Fine from Brown Sheep Company (80% cotton and 20% merino wool; 1.75 oz/50 g; 222 yds/203 m) ❨**2**❩

A   Color CF-550 Mariner Blue

T-shirt: 4 (5, 6, 7) skeins

Cowl: 1 skein

B   Color CF-570 Malibu Blue

T-shirt: 4 (4, 5, 6) skeins

Cowl: 1 skein

Size 3 (3.25 mm) needles or size required to obtain gauge

Size 3 (3.25 mm) circular needle (16")

GAUGE

26 sts and 34 rows = 4" in St st

T-SHIRT INSTRUCTIONS

back

With A, cable CO 117 (130, 143, 156) sts.

Rows 1–6: Beg with knit on RS, work in St st.

Row 7 (RS): K2 (1, 2, 1), *YO, K2tog, rep from * to last st, K1. This row is fold line for hem.

Rows 8–14: Cont in St st.

Row 15: Change to B and cont in St st.

Cont alternating colors every 6 rows until work measures 14 (14½, 15, 15½)" from fold line of hem (row 7), approx through row 126 (130, 134, 140).

Shape armholes: BO 5 (6, 6, 6) sts at beg of next 2 rows. Dec 1 st, then BO 2 (2, 3, 3) sts at beg of next 2 rows. Dec 1 st, then BO 1 (1, 1, 2) st at beg of next 2 rows—97 (108, 119, 130) sts. Work even to armhole depth of 7 (7½, 8, 8½)", approx through row 185 (193, 202, 212).

Shape neck and shoulders:

Row 186 (194, 203, 213): Work 36 (40, 43, 48) sts, BO center 25 (28, 33, 34) sts for neck, finish row. Work both sides at same time. BO 8 (9, 10, 11) sts at shoulder edge, work to neck opening, attach second ball of yarn to second st at neck edge, dec 1 st, then BO 5 (6, 6, 7) sts at beg of neck edge, work to end. Next row, with 1 ball of yarn BO 8 (9, 10, 11) sts at shoulder edge, and with other ball of yarn dec 1, then BO 5 (6, 6, 7) sts at beg of neck edge. Cont in this manner with 2 balls of yarn, on

next row, dec 1 st, then BO 8 (9, 10, 11) sts at shoulder edge and dec 1 st, then BO 3 (3, 3, 4) sts at beg of neck edge. On next row, dec 1 st, then BO 8 (9, 10, 11) sts at shoulder edge and dec 1 st, then BO 3 (3, 3, 4) sts at beg of neck edge. On beg of final 2 rows, dec 1 st, then BO 8 (9, 10, 11) sts at shoulder edge.

front

Work as for back, cont past armhole shaping until front measures 18¾ (19¾, 20½, 21½)" from fold line of hem (row 7), approx through row 165 (173, 181, 189).

Shape neck:

Row 166 (174, 182, 190): Work 38 (42, 47, 52) sts, BO center 21 (24, 25, 26) sts, finish row. Dec 1 st, then BO 3 (3, 4, 4) sts at beg of neck edge over next 2 rows. Dec 1 st, then BO 1 (1, 2, 2) st at beg of neck edge over next 2 rows. **For Extra Large only,** dec 1 st, then BO 1 st at neck edge over next 2 rows. **For all sizes,** dec 1 st at beg of neck edge over next 12 (14, 14, 14) rows.

Shape shoulders as for back.

sleeves

With A, cable CO 48 (56, 62, 66) sts.

Work as for back through row 20.

Shape sleeves:

Row 21: Inc 1 st after and before selvage st using M1 inc. Work this inc every 8 rows 16 more times—82 (90, 96, 100) sts. Work to 17" from row 7, approx through row 152.

Shape caps: BO 5 (6, 6, 6) sts at beg of next 2 rows. Dec 1 st, then BO 2 (2, 3, 3) sts at beg of next 2 rows. Dec 1 st, then BO 1 (1, 1, 2) st at beg of next 2 rows. Dec 1 st each edge

EOR a total of 8 (10, 12, 13) times. Dec 1 st at each edge every row 9 times. Dec 1 st, then BO 1 st at beg of next 2 rows. Dec 1 st, then BO 2 sts at beg of next 2 rows. BO rem 18 (20, 20, 20) sts on next row.

finishing

Meticulously block to measurements. Block hems folded into place as they will be when garment is finished.

Seam shoulders using invisible horizontal seaming.

Neckband: Using 16" circular needle, PU even number of sts in gauge around neck edge. Work 4 rnds knitting all sts. **Rnd 5:** (K2tog, YO) around. **Rnds 6–9:** Knit. BO loosely on next rnd. Seam sleeves into armholes using invisible vertical to horizontal seaming.

Seam sides and underarms using invisible vertical seaming for St st.

Whipstitch hems at bottom edge, cuff, and neck into place.

COWL INSTRUCTIONS

Using circular needle and A, cable CO 156 sts. You may find it helpful to CO using straight needles and work first row onto circular needle to avoid twisting.

Rnds 1–3: *K2, P2; rep from * around.

Rnds 4–6: Knit.

Change to B, cont to knit all rnds, alternating colors every 6 rnds until cowl neck measures approx 6½" or desired length. End with A, knit 3 rnds, then work 2 rnds in K2, P2 ribbing, and BO in patt on next rnd.

Weave in all ends and steam block.

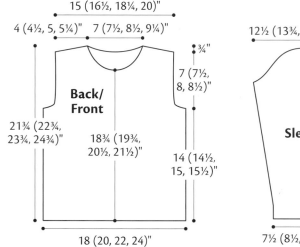

15 (16½, 18¼, 20)"
4 (4½, 5, 5¼)"   7 (7½, 8½, 9¼)"
¾"
Back/Front
7 (7½, 8, 8½)"
21¾ (22¾, 23¾, 24¾)"   18¾ (19¾, 20½, 21½)"
14 (14½, 15, 15½)"
18 (20, 22, 24)"

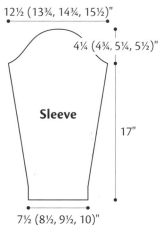

12½ (13¾, 14¾, 15½)"
4¼ (4¾, 5¼, 5½)"
Sleeve
17"
7½ (8½, 9½, 10)"

mock pleat and rib
TURTLENECK and SKIRT

Skill Level: Easy ◀■□□

Size: Small (Medium, Large, Extra Large)

Finished Measurements

Turtleneck Bust: 41 (44½, 50½, 54)"

Turtleneck Length: 25 (25¼, 25½, 25¾)"

Skirt Waist: 29 (31, 33, 35)" (skirt is designed to be worn slightly below the waist)

Skirt Length: 21 (22, 23, 24)"

MATERIALS

Gems Topaz from Louet Sales (100% merino wool; 100 g; 168 yds) in color Sandalwood (■4■)

    Cardigan: 6 (7, 8, 9) skeins

    Skirt: 4 (5, 6, 7) skeins

Size 8 (5 mm) needles or size required to obtain gauge

Size 8 (5 mm) circular needle (16") for neck

1 package (1 yd) nonroll, ¾"-wide elastic for skirt

GAUGE

18 sts and 28 rows = 4" in 3 x 4 ribbing patt when blocked

PATTERN STITCHES

Mock Pleat
(Multiple of 8 sts)

Row 1 (RS): *K7, P1; rep from *.

Row 2 (WS): K3, *P1, K7; rep from * to last 5 sts, P1, K4.

Rep these 2 rows.

3 x 4 Ribbing
(Multiple of 7 sts)

Row 1 (RS): *K3, P4; rep from *.

Row 2 (WS): *K4, P3; rep from *.

Rep these 2 rows.

SELVAGE STITCHES

Selvage stitches are identified in parentheses in the first two rows of the pattern and are included in the instructions for the following rows without being labeled as such.

TURTLENECK INSTRUCTIONS

back

Cable CO 122 (138, 154, 162) sts. Work mock pleat edging as follows.

Row 1 (RS): K1 (selvage st), *K7, P1, rep from * to last st, K1 (selvage st).

Row 2: K1 (selvage st), K3, *P1, K7, rep from * to last 6 sts, P1, K4, K1 (selvage st).

Rep rows 1 and 2 for a total of 28 rows.

Here you will find easy stitching with only knits and purls, yet the simple ribbing and crisp mock pleats provide wonderful texture. These versatile pieces can be dressed up or down. Together or separate, there's a lot of wardrobe magic and mileage for you.

Row 29: Knit all sts and dec 29 (38, 40, 41) sts evenly spaced using K2tog—93 (100, 114, 121) sts.

Rows 30, 33, and 34: Knit.

Rows 31, 32, 35, and 36: K1, purl to last st, K1.

Row 37: K1, P2, *K3, P4; rep from * to last 6 sts, K3, P2, K1.

Row 38: K1, K2, *P3, K4; rep from * to last 6 sts, P3, K2, K1.

Cont in ribbing as est until work measures 17"; approx 119 rows.

Shape armholes: BO 4 (4, 5, 6) sts at beg of next 2 rows. Dec 1, then BO 1 (2, 2, 2) st at beg of next 2 rows. Dec 1 st at each edge EOR 0 (1, 3, 3) times—81 (84, 92, 97) sts. Work even to armhole depth of 7¼ (7½, 7¾, 8)", approx through row 168 (170, 172, 174).

Shape neck and shoulders: Work 32 (33, 37, 39) sts in patt, BO center 17 (18, 18, 19) sts, work in patt to end. Work both sides at same time. BO 7 (8, 9, 9) sts at shoulder edge, work to neck opening; attach second ball of yarn in second st at neck edge, dec 1 st, then BO 4 (4, 4, 5) sts at beg of neck edge, work to end. On next row, with 1 ball of yarn, BO 7 (8, 9, 9) sts at shoulder edge, and with second ball of yarn, dec 1 st, then BO 4 (4, 4, 5) sts at beg of neck edge of same row. Cont in this manner with 2 balls of yarn, on next row dec 1 st, then BO 7 (7, 8, 9) sts at shoulder edge, and dec 1 st, then BO 2 (2, 3, 3) sts at beg of neck edge. On next row, dec 1 st, then BO 7 (7, 8, 9) sts at shoulder edge, and dec 1 st, then BO 2 (2, 3, 3) sts at beg of neck edge. On last 2 rows, dec 1 st, then BO 8 (8, 9, 9) sts at shoulder edge.

front

Work as for back, cont past armhole shaping until front measures 23¼ (23½, 23¾, 24)", approx through row 162 (164, 166, 168).

Shape neck: Work in patt across 33 (34, 38, 40) sts, BO center 15 (16, 16, 17) sts, work in patt to end. Work 33 (34, 38, 40) sts in patt; attach second ball of yarn to second st at neck edge, dec 1 st, then BO 3 (3, 4, 4) sts at beg of neck edge, work to end. On next row, work 29 (30, 33, 35) sts, dec 1 st, then BO 3 (3, 4, 4) sts at beg of neck edge, work to end. Next 2 rows, dec 1 st, then BO 2 (2,

2, 3) sts at beg of neck edge. Next 4 rows, dec 1 st at beg of neck edge and AT SAME TIME, beg shoulder shaping as for back.

sleeves

With separate balls of yarn, cable CO 42 (50, 58, 58) sts for both sleeves at same time. Work rows 1–20 as for back.

Row 21: Knit and dec 10 (11, 12, 12) sts evenly spaced using K2tog—32 (39, 46, 46) sts.

Work rows 22–27 as rows 30–35 for back.

Row 28: K1, M1 pw, P15, M1 pw, P15, M1 pw, K1—35 (42, 49, 49) sts.

Row 29: K1, P1, *K3, P4; rep from * to last 5 sts, K3, P1, K1.

Row 30: K2, *P3, K4; rep from * to last 5 sts, P3, K2.

Cont in ribbing as est.

Shape sleeves: Beg on row 35 (35, 37, 37), inc 1 st at each edge inside selvage sts using M1 kw or M1 pw as appropriate to patt. Work this inc every 6 rows another 11 (3, 0, 0) times, then every 8 rows 2 (8, 11, 11) times—63 (66, 71, 71) sts and 126 rows.

Shape caps: BO 4 (4, 5, 6) sts at beg of next 2 rows. Dec 1 st, then BO 1 (2, 2, 2) st at beg of next 2 rows. Dec 1 st at beg of next 10 (11, 14, 18) rows. Dec 1 st at each edge of next 9 (9, 9, 6) rows. Dec 1 st, then BO 1 st at beg of next 2 rows. Dec 1 st, then BO 2 sts at beg of next 2 rows. BO rem 13 sts.

finishing

Meticulously steam block all pieces above mock pleats to measurements. In order not to flatten them, do not pin or block mock pleats. Pin and block only above pleats.

Seam shoulders using invisible horizontal seaming.

Neck: Using circular needle, PU 84 (84, 91, 98) sts.

Rnds 1 and 2: Purl.

Rnd 3: *P4, K3; rep from *. Rep rnd 3 for a total of 18 rnds, and BO in patt on next rnd. If you prefer mock turtleneck or shorter turtleneck, work fewer rnds.

Sew sleeves into armholes using invisible vertical to horizontal seaming.

Sew side seams and underarm seams using invisible vertical seaming.

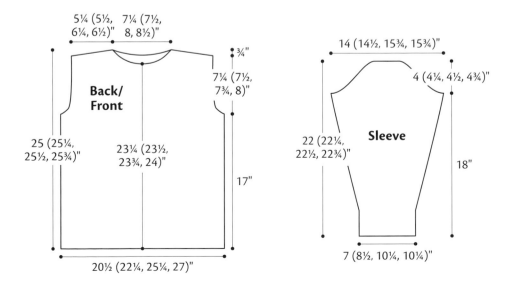

SKIRT INSTRUCTIONS

front and back

Make 2 pieces the same.

Work as for turtleneck back to length of 13 (14, 15, 16)", ending with WS row, approx through row 90 (98, 104, 112), or work to desired length.

Shape hip: Cont in patt as est, dec 1 st at each edge using ssk at beg of row and K2tog at end of row every 4 rows a total of 14 (13, 8, 7) times and every 2 rows a total of 0 (2, 12, 14) times. On last dec, row 143 (151, 157, 165), change to St st—65 (70, 74, 79) sts.

Work another 4 rows in St st.

Next row: Knit. This forms fold line for waistband.

Work 4 more rows in St st and BO all sts kw on next row.

finishing

Meticulously steam block front and back above mock pleats to measurements. In order not to flatten them, do not pin or block mock pleats. Pin and block only above pleats.

Seam sides using invisible vertical seaming.

Fold waistband at fold line and whipstitch into place on inside of garment, leaving a small 1" to 2" opening. Attach a safety pin to end of waist elastic and work through waistband, or position appropriate length of elastic in place as you seam. Remove safety pin. Seam edges of elastic. Finish closing remainder of waistband.

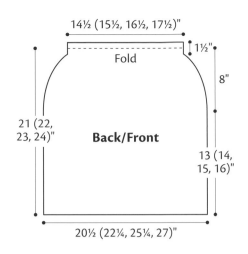

14½ (15½, 16½, 17½)"

1½"

Fold

8"

21 (22, 23, 24)"

Back/Front

13 (14, 15, 16)"

20½ (22¼, 25¼, 27)"

eyelet and ruffle
CARDIGAN and SHELL

Skill Level: Easy ◖■□□

Size: Small (Medium, Large, Extra Large)

Finished Measurements

Cardigan Bust: 33½ (35¾, 39½, 42¾)"

Cardigan Length: 21 (22, 23, 24)"

Shell Bust: 32½ (36½, 41, 45)"

Shell Length: 18 (19½, 20¾, 22¼)"

A WORD ABOUT MEASUREMENTS

Do not misinterpret the cardigan finished-bust measurements to indicate that this cardigan runs small. It is a cutaway cardigan that does not close in front and lies more open on the body.

MATERIALS

Endless Summer Collection Sonata from Elann.com (100% mercerized cotton; 50 g; 115 yds/106 m) in color 460 white ❸

Cardigan: 9 (10, 11, 12) skeins

Shell: 4 (5, 6, 7) skeins

Piece of smaller-gauge yarn to hold stitches

Size 6 (4 mm) needles or size required to obtain gauge

Size 6 (4 mm) circular needle (29") for neck and front edging

GAUGE

19 sts and 28 rows = 4" in main patt and St st when blocked

PATTERN STITCHES

Single Eyelet Rib

See chart on page 29.

Used in all edging and on fronts and back.

(Multiple of 5 sts + 2 sts)

Rows 1 and 5 (RS): P2, *K3, P2; rep from *.

Row 2 and all WS rows: *K2, P3; rep from * to last 2 sts, K2.

Row 3: P2, *K2tog, YO, K1, P2; rep from *.

Row 7: P2, *K1, YO, ssk, P2; rep from *.

Row 8: *K2, P3; rep from * to last 2 sts, K2.

Rep rows 1–8 for patt.

Double Eyelet Rib

See chart on page 29.

Used at center of back and sleeves and at front outer edges.

(Multiple of 7 sts + 2 sts)

Row 1 (RS): P2, *K5, P2; rep from *.

Rows 2 and 4 (WS): *K2, P5; rep from * to last 2 sts, K2.

Row 3: P2, *K2tog, YO, K1, YO, ssk, P2; rep from *.

Rep rows 1–4 for patt.

SELVAGE STITCHES

Selvage stitches are identified in parentheses in the first two rows of the pattern and are included in the instructions for the following rows without being labeled as such.

CARDIGAN INSTRUCTIONS

back

Cable CO 104 (109, 119, 129) sts. Work ribbing as follows.

Rows 1 and 5 (RS): K1 (selvage st), P2, *K3, P2; rep from * to last st, K1 (selvage st).

Rows 2, 4, and 6: K1 (selvage st), K2, *P3, K2; rep from * to last st, K1 (selvage st).

Row 3: K1, P2, *K2tog, YO, K1, P2; rep from * to last st, K1.

Row 7 (dec row): K1, P2tog, *K2tog, YO, K1, P2tog; rep from * to last st, K1—83 (87, 95, 103) sts.

Rows 8 and 10: K2, *P3, K1; rep from * to last st, K1.

Row 9: K1, P1, *K3, P1; rep from * to last st, K1.

Row 11: K1, P1, *K2tog, YO, K1, P1; rep from * to last st, K1.

Rows 12–14: Rep rows 8, 9, and 10.

Change to main patt as follows.

Row 15: K1, K31 (33, 37, 41), P2, K2tog, YO, K1, P2, K2tog, YO, K1, YO, ssk, P2, K1, YO, ssk, P2, K31 (33, 37, 41), K1.

Rows 16, 18, 20, and 22: K1, P31 (33, 37, 41), K2, P3, K2, P5, K2, P3, K2, P31 (33, 37, 41), K1.

Rows 17 and 21: K1, K31 (33, 37, 41), P2, K3, P2, K5, P2, K3, P2, K31 (33, 37, 41), K1.

Row 19: K1, K31 (33, 37, 41), P2, K1, YO, ssk, P2, K2tog, YO, K1, YO, ssk, P2, K2tog, YO, K1, P2, K31 (33, 37, 41), K1.

Rep rows 15–22 until work measures 13½ (14, 14½, 15)" from beg, approx 95 (99, 101, 105) total rows.

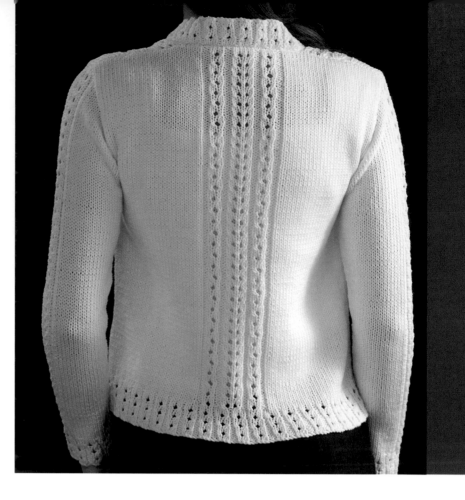

Shape armholes: BO 3 (4, 4, 5) sts at beg of next 2 rows. Dec 1 st, then BO 1 (1, 2, 2) st at beg of next 2 rows—73 (75, 81, 87) sts. Cont in est patt until armhole measures 7 (7½, 8, 8½)", approx 144 (151, 157, 164) total rows.

Shape shoulders: BO 7 (7, 8, 8) sts at beg of next 2 rows. Dec 1 st, then BO 6 (7, 7, 8) sts at beg of next 2 rows. Dec 1 st, then BO 7 (7, 8, 9) sts at beg of next 2 rows. BO rem 29 (29, 31, 33) neck sts, working no YO or dec in single or double eyelet ribbing on last 2 rows.

fronts

With separate balls of yarn, cable CO 39 (44, 49, 54) sts for right and left front at same time. Work rows 1–14 as for back, note that right and left front are the same and do not yet require reverse shaping—31 (35, 39, 43) sts after row 7.

Row 15

Left front: K18 (22, 26, 30), P2, K2tog, YO, K1, P2, K2tog, YO, K1, YO, ssk, K1.

Right front: K1, K2tog, YO, K1, YO, ssk, P2, K1, YO, ssk, P2, K18 (22, 26, 30).

Rows 16, 18, 20, and 22

Right front: K1, P17 (21, 25, 29), K2, P3, K2, P5, K1.

Left front: K1, P5, K2, P3, K2, P17 (21, 25, 29), K1.

Rows 17 and 21

Left front: K18 (22, 26, 30), P2, K3, P2, K6.

Right front: K6, P2, K3, P2, K18 (22, 26, 30).

Row 19

Left front: K18 (22, 26, 30), P2, K1, YO, ssk, P2, K2tog, YO, K1, YO, ssk, K1.

Right front: K1, K2tog, YO, K1, YO, ssk, P2, K2tog, YO, K1, P2, K18 (22, 26, 30).

Rep rows 15–22 until work measures 12", ending on WS row; approx 84 rows total.

Shape neck:

Row 85 (dec row)

Left front: K16 (20, 24, 28), K2tog, P2, K3, P2, K6.

Right front: K6, P2, K3, P2, K2tog tbl, K16 (20, 24, 28).

Cont in patt as est, rep dec row every 16 (12, 10, 10) rows 3 (5, 6, 7) times. AT SAME TIME shape armholes and shoulders as for back.

sleeves

With separate balls of yarn, cable CO 54 (54, 59, 59) sts for both sleeves at same time. Work rows 1–14 as for back—43 (43, 47, 47) sts after row 7.

Row 15: K17 (17, 19, 19), P2, K2tog, YO, K1, YO, ssk, P2, K17 (17, 19, 19).

Rows 16 and 18: K1, P16 (16, 18, 18), K2, P5, K2, P16 (16, 18, 18), K1.

Row 17: K17 (17, 19, 19), P2, K5, P2, K17 (17, 19, 19).

Cont in est patt.

Shape sleeves: Beg on row 37, inc 1 st at each edge using M1 kw inside selvage sts. Work this inc every 10 (8, 10, 8) rows 8 (9, 8, 10) more times—61 (63, 65, 69) sts. Work even to 18" from beg; approx 126 total rows.

Shape caps: BO 3 (4, 4, 5) sts at beg of next 2 rows. Dec 1 st, then BO 1 (1, 2, 2) st at beg of next 2 rows. Dec 1 st at each edge EOR 3 (4, 6, 7) times. Dec 1 st at each edge every row 10 (9, 7, 7) times. Dec 1 st, then BO 1 st at beg of next 2 rows. Dec 1 st, then BO 2 sts at beg of next 2 rows. BO rem 15 sts.

finishing

Meticulously block pieces to measurements.

Sew shoulder seams using invisible horizontal seaming.

Sew sleeves into armholes using invisible vertical to horizontal seaming.

Sew side seams and underarm seams using invisible vertical seaming.

Neck and front edging: Using circular needle, cable CO 309 (319, 329, 344) sts. Work rows 1–10 as for back—247 (255, 263, 275) sts after row 7. Thread a tapestry needle in contrasting-color, smaller-gauge

yarn and sl needle through each st on circular needle, transferring each st from circular needle to strand of yarn.

Pin and block edging to 1½" x 52 (53¾, 55¼, 58)". Transfer these live sts back to circular needle. PU corresponding number of sts around left front edge, back of neck, and right front edge, with RS facing you. Work 3-needle BO to attach edging. Note that if you BO too tightly the edging will pucker. At lower border of edging where it attaches to bottom of sweater, pin to ironing board one side at a time, with RS facing down. Even and straighten front bottom edges by lightly pressing and steaming with iron. Also pin inside seam to flatten and inside edge of garment. Open those seams by lightly pressing and steaming.

Single eyelet rib

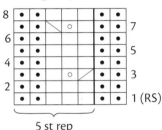

5 st rep

Double eyelet rib

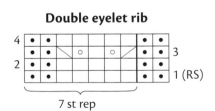

7 st rep

Key

☐ K on RS, P on WS
• P on RS, K on WS
◿ K2tog
◺ Ssk
○ YO

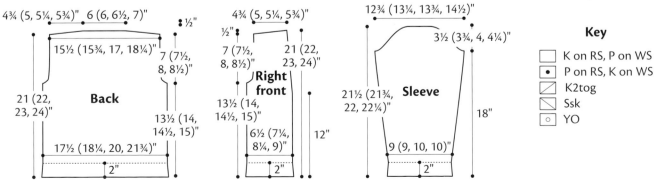

4¾ (5, 5¼, 5¾)" 6 (6, 6½, 7)" ½"

15½ (15¾, 17, 18¼)" 7 (7½, 8, 8½)"

Back

21 (22, 23, 24)"

13½ (14, 14½, 15)"

17½ (18¼, 20, 21¾)" 2"

4¾ (5, 5¼, 5¾)" ½"

7 (7½, 8, 8½)" 21 (22, 23, 24)"

Right front

13½ (14, 14½, 15)"

6½ (7¼, 8¼, 9)" 12" 2"

12¾ (13¼, 13¾, 14½)"

3½ (3¾, 4, 4¼)"

21½ (21¾, 22, 22¼)" **Sleeve** 18"

9 (9, 10, 10)" 2"

SHELL INSTRUCTIONS

front

Cable CO 75 (85, 95, 105) sts.

Rows 1 and 5 (RS): K1, P1 (2, 1, 2), *K3, P1; rep from * to last 1 (2, 1, 2) st, P0 (1, 0, 1), K1.

Rows 2 and 4: K2 (3, 2, 3), *P3, K1; rep from * to last 1 (2, 1, 2) st, K1 (2, 1, 2).

Row 3: K1, P1 (2, 1, 2), *K2tog, YO, K1, P1; rep from * to last 1 (2, 1, 2) sts, P0 (1, 0, 1), K1.

Row 6: K1, M1 pw, purl to last st, M1 pw, K1—77 (87, 97, 107) sts.

Work in St st, knit all RS rows and purl all WS rows until work measures 11½ (12, 12½, 13)" from beg; approx 81 (84, 88, 91) total rows.

Shape armholes: BO 4 (4, 5, 6) sts at beg of next 2 rows. Dec 1 st, then BO 1 (2, 2, 2) st at beg of next 2 rows—65 (73, 81, 89) sts. Work 11 (18, 24, 31) more rows in St st.

Change patt:

Row 97 (107, 117, 127): K2, P1, *K3, P1; rep from * to last 2 sts, K2.

Row 98 (108, 118, 128): K1, P1, K1, *P3, K1; rep from * to last 2 sts, P1, K1.

Row 99 (109, 119, 129): K2, P1, *K2tog, YO, K1, P1; rep from * to last 2 sts, K2.

Row 100 (110, 120, 130): Rep row 98 (108, 118, 128).

Row 101 (111, 121, 131): Rep row 97 (107, 117, 127).

Shape neck:

Row 102 (112, 122, 132): K1, *M1 pw, P1, M1 kw, K1, M1 pw, P2; rep from *, M1 pw, P1, M1 kw, K2, BO center 41 (49, 57, 65) sts, K2, *M1 kw, P1, M1 pw, P2, M1 pw, K1; rep from *, M1 kw, P1, M1 pw, K1. Note that 20 sts on each side form shoulder straps.

Row 103 (113, 123, 133): K1, P1, K1, (P2, K1, K2tog, YO, K2) twice, P2, K1, attach second ball of yarn, K1, P2, (K1, K2tog, YO, K2, P2) twice, K1, P1, K1.

Row 104 (114, 124, 134): K2, P1, (K2, P5) twice, K3, and for second side of shoulder strap K3, (P5, K2) twice, P1, K2.

Row 105 (115, 125, 135): K1, P1, K1, (P2, K5) twice, P2, K1, and for second side of shoulder K1, P2, (K5, P2) twice, K1, P1, K1.

Row 106 (116, 126, 136): Rep row 104 (114, 124, 134).

Rep rows 103 (113, 123, 133)–106 (116, 126, 136) 12 times, through row 154 (164, 174, 184) OR to desired length for your proportion. Leave sts on needle.

back

Work as for front through row 101 (111, 121, 131).

Row 102 (112, 122, 133): K1, P1, (K1, P3) twice, K2, BO center 41 (49, 57, 65) sts, work rem st in patt and leave on needle. There are 12 sts on each side for joining to shoulder straps.

finishing

Meticulously block pieces to measurements.

Shoulder straps: Transfer back of garment to another needle to face correct way. With RS of front and back tog, use 3-needle BO to seam shoulder straps to back of garment. The 20-st edge of front strap will require 8 decs during 3-needle BO to 12 sts on the back. Work decs on front sts only and 1 corresponding st on back tog and BO as follows.

Row 155: BO each st as you work sts in this manner: K2tog, K1, K2tog twice, K1, K2tog 3 times, K1, K2tog twice, K1. Reverse this shaping for left front strap. (K1, K2tog twice, K1, K2tog 3 times, K1, K2tog twice, K1, K2tog).

Sew side seams and underarm seams using invisible vertical seaming.

Edging: PU sts in gauge from lower edge of shoulder strap, underarm, to lower edge of opposite shoulder strap. Knit and BO in same row to finish this edge.

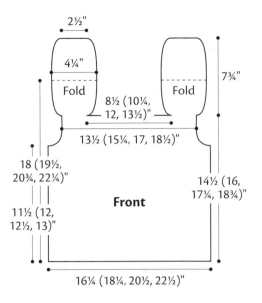

moss and feather faggot
CARDIGAN and SHELL

Skill Level: Intermediate ◖■■◻

Size: Small (Medium, Large, Extra Large)

Finished Measurements

Cardigan Bust: 35½ (39, 42½, 46)"

Cardigan Length: 21¾ (22¾, 23¾, 24¾)"

Shell Bust: 28½ (32, 36½, 40)" (Note that the close-fitting shell will open up; the smallest size will fit size 32" bust.)

Shell Length: 19 (19¾, 20½, 21¼)"

MATERIALS

Cotton Classic from Tahki Imports (100% mercerized cotton; 1.75 oz/50g; 108 yds/100 m) in color 3882 ⊙3

    Cardigan: 8 (9, 10, 11) skeins

    Shell: 4 (5, 6, 7) skeins

Size 6 (4 mm) needles or size required to obtain gauge

Size 6 (4 mm) circular needle (16") for shell neck and armhole edging

GAUGE

18 sts and 28 rows = 4" in combination of moss and feather faggot patt, when blocked

PATTERN STITCHES

Moss Stitch

See chart on page 35.

(Over an even number of sts)

Rows 1 and 2: *K1, P1; rep from *.

Rows 3 and 4: *P1, K1; rep from *.

Rep rows 1–4 for patt.

Feather Faggot

See chart on page 35.

(Multiple of 4 sts)

All rows: *K1, YO, P2tog, K1; rep from *.

CARDIGAN INSTRUCTIONS

back

Cable CO 86 (94, 102, 110) sts. Work 12 rows in moss st with 1 selvage st at each edge.

Row 13 (RS): K1 (selvage st), *4 sts in moss st, 4 sts in feather faggot st; rep from * to last 5 sts, 4 sts in moss st, K1 (selvage st).

Rows 14–28 (14–30, 14–32, 14–34): Cont in patt as est.

Row 29 (31, 33, 35): Dec 1 st at each edge inside selvage sts, and work this dec every 28 (30, 30, 30) rows twice more—80 (88, 96, 104) sts.

Work even in patt as est until back measures 14 (14½, 15, 15½)" from beg; approx 97 (101, 103, 107) rows.

This body-skimming, cropped, three-quarter sleeve cardigan is perfect for warm weather with its open-stitched stripes in the feather faggot pattern. The body-conscious shell features a V-shaped accent at the neckline to complement the cardigan, and a flattering, open-stitched striped back to keep you cool.

Row 98 (102, 104, 108): Work last 4 sts of row in feather faggot st as K1, P2, K1 in preparation for armhole shaping.

Shape armholes: BO 4 (4, 5, 6) sts at beg of next 2 rows and work last 4 sts in feather faggot st of first of these 2 rows as for row 98 (102, 104, 108). Dec 1 st, then BO 1 (2, 2, 2) st at beg of next 2 rows—68 (74, 80, 86) sts. Work even in patt as est until armhole is 7 (7½, 8, 8½)", approx through row 148 (154, 160, 168).

Shape shoulders: BO 6 (7, 7, 8) sts at beg of next 2 rows. Dec 1 st, then BO 6 (6, 7, 8) sts at beg of next 2 rows. Dec 1 st, then BO 6 (7, 8, 8) sts at beg of next 2 rows. BO rem 28 (30, 32, 34) sts.

front

With separate balls of yarn, cable CO 44 (48, 52, 56) sts for right and left front at same time. Work 12 rows of edging as for back.

Row 13 (RS): (K1, P1) 0 (1, 0, 1) times, *4 sts in moss st, 4 sts in feather faggot st; rep from *, end last 4 (6, 4, 6) sts in moss st.

Cont in patt as est, working outer-edge shaping as for back, which will be 3-st dec on each side of front. Work in patt to 10", approx through row 70 and AT SAME TIME beg neck shaping as follows, and shape armholes and shoulders as for back.

Shape neck: Work neck decs on indicated RS rows as follows. Note that neck decs are worked within moss st vertical bands of front, beg at outer edge and working inward.

Row 71

Left front: Work 34 (36, 42, 44) sts in patt to last 8 (10, 8, 10) sts, K1, YO, P2tog twice, work 3 (5, 3, 5) sts in moss st.

Right front: Work 3 (5, 3, 5) sts in moss st, K2tog, YO, P2tog, K1, cont in est patt to end of row.

Row 79

Left front: Work 33 (35, 41, 43) sts in patt to last 8 (10, 8, 10) sts, K2tog, YO, P2tog, (P1, K1) 2 (3, 2, 3) times. Note that neck decs are worked on either side of the YO, P2tog of the feather faggot patt st so that moss st bands will narrow as neck decs are worked, and to maintain patt, the K1 sts on either side of the YO, P2tog are gradually omitted, which must be reflected in following rows.

Right front: (P1, K1) 2 (3, 2, 3) times, YO, P2tog twice, work in patt to end.

Row 87

Left front: Work 25 (27, 33, 35) sts in patt to last 14 (16, 14, 16) sts, K1, YO, P2tog twice, K1, P1, K1, YO, K2tog, (P1, K1) 2 (3, 2, 3) times—38 (42, 47, 51) sts.

Right front: (P1, K1) 2 (3, 2, 3) times, YO, P2tog, P1, K1, P1, K2tog, YO, P2tog, K1, work in patt to end.

Row 95

Left front: Work 24 (26, 32, 34) sts in patt to last 14 (16, 14, 16) sts, K2tog, YO, P2tog, (P1, K1) twice, YO, P2tog, (P1, K1) 2 (3, 2, 3) times.

Right front: (P1, K1) 2 (3, 2, 3) times, YO, P2tog, (P1, K1) twice, YO, P2tog twice, K1, P1, K1, work to end—37 (41, 45, 49) sts.

AT SAME TIME as neck shaping, on row 99 (103, 105, 109), shape armholes as for back.

Row 103

Left front: Work 12 (16, 26, 28) sts in patt, YO, P2tog twice, K1, P1, K1, (YO, P2tog, [P1, K1] twice) twice, (P1, K1) 0 (1, 0, 1) times.

Right front: (P1, K1) 0 (1, 0, 1) times, ([P1, K1] twice, YO, P2tog) twice, P1, K1, P1, K2tog, YO, P2tog, work in patt to end—30 (36, 44, 48) sts.

Note that for medium, sts rem will be 36 after row 104 armhole shaping.

Row 111

Left front: Work 10 (11, 16, 17) sts in est patt, K2tog, (YO, P2tog, [P1, K1] twice) 3 times, (P1, K1) 0 (1, 0, 1) times.

Right front: (P1, K1) 0 (1, 0, 1) times, ([P1, K1] twice, YO, P2tog) 3 times, P2tog, work in est patt to end of row—29 (32, 35, 38) sts.

Row 119

Left front: Work 6 (7, 12, 13) sts in est patt, P2tog, K1, P1, K1, (YO, P2tog, [P1, K1] twice) 3 times, (P1, K1) 0 (1, 0, 1) times.

Right front: (P1, K1) 0 (1, 0, 1) times, ([P1, K1] twice, YO, P2tog) 3 times, P1, K1, P1, K2tog, YO, P2tog, (K1, P1) twice, work in patt to end—28 (31, 34, 37) sts.

Row 127

Left front: Work 20 (21, 26, 27) sts as est, P2tog, YO, P2tog, (P1, K1) twice, (P1, K1) 0 (1, 0, 1) times.

Right front: (P1, K1) 0 (1, 0, 1) times, (P1, K1) twice, YO, P2tog, K2tog, P1, K1, work in patt to end—27 (30, 33, 36) sts.

Row 135

Left front: Work 14 (15, 20, 21) sts as est, P2tog, (YO, P2tog, P1, K1, P1) twice, P1, (K1, P1) 0 (1, 0, 1) times.

Right front: (P1, K1) 0 (1, 0, 1) times, P1, (K1, P1, K1, YO, P2tog) twice, K2tog, P1, K1, work in patt to end—26 (29, 32, 35) sts.

Row 143

Left front: Work 8 (9, 14, 15) sts as est, K2tog, (YO, P2tog, P1, K1, P1) twice, YO, P2tog, (P1, K1) 2 (3, 2, 3) times.

Right front: (P1, K1) 2 (3, 2, 3) times, (YO, P2tog, K1, P1, K1) twice, YO, P2tog, K2tog, work in patt to end—25 (28, 31, 34) sts.

After shoulder shaping, 5 (6, 7, 8) sts rem. Cont to work back neck edge in moss st only to length of 3⅛ (3¼, 3½, 3¾)" and leave sts on needle for grafting to other edge as grafting will give smoothest seam for center back of neckline. Note that if back neck edges are knit to too long a length, neck will not lie correctly even with fullness eased in.

sleeves

With separate balls of yarn, cable CO 44 (48, 52, 56) sts for both sleeves. Work edging and est patt as for front.

Shape sleeves: Beg row 15 (17, 19, 15), inc 1 st each edge inside selvage sts using M1 kw or M1 pw as appropriate to maintain moss st patt for all incs and rep this inc another 5 (5, 5, 6) times every 14 rows—56 (60, 64, 70) sts. Work until sleeve measures 14 (14½, 15, 15½)" from beg; approx 98 (102, 104, 108) total rows.

Shape caps: BO 4 (4, 5, 6) sts at beg of next 2 rows. Dec 1 st, then BO 1 (2, 2, 2) st at beg of next 2 rows. Work 2 rows even. Dec 1 st at each edge every third row 3 times, then EOR 6 (7, 8, 9) times. Dec 1 st, then BO 1 st at beg of next 2 rows. Dec 1 st, then BO 2 sts at beg of next 2 rows. BO rem 16 (16, 16, 18) sts.

finishing

Meticulously block all pieces to measurements, opening up YO sts.

Seam shoulders using invisible horizontal seaming.

Graft center back of neck live sts tog and sew back of neck edging in place using invisible horizontal seaming.

Sew sleeves into armholes using invisible vertical to horizontal seaming.

Sew side seams and underarm seams using invisible vertical seaming.

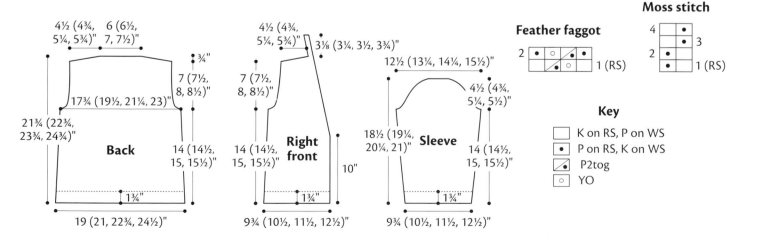

SHELL INSTRUCTIONS

front and back

(Worked in one piece from lower front to lower back.)

Cable CO 64 (72, 82, 90) sts. Work edging as for cardigan back and cont to work in moss st through row 24 (26, 28, 30).

Shape waist: Beg row 25 (27, 29, 31), dec 1 st at each edge inside selvage sts, then rep this dec 3 more times every 6 rows. Beg row 49 (51, 53, 55), inc 1 st using M1 kw or M1 pw as appropriate to patt at each edge inside selvage sts, then rep this inc 3 more times every 6 rows. Work even to 12 (12½, 13, 13½)", through approx row 84 (88, 90, 94).

Shape armholes: BO 3 (3, 4, 4) sts at beg of next 2 rows. Dec 1 st, then BO 0 (1, 1, 2) sts at beg of next 2 rows—56 (62, 70, 76) sts. Work even for 4 (6, 8, 10) more rows.

Work neck detail on RS rows as follows.

Row 93 (99, 103, 109): K1 (selvage st), work 25 (28, 32, 35) sts in moss st, work 4 sts in feather faggot st, work 25 (28, 32, 35) sts in moss st, K1 (selvage st). Cont these patts as est until next addition of feather faggot neck detail on following rows.

Row 99 (105, 109, 115): K1, work 21 (24, 28, 31) sts in moss st, YO, P2tog, 2 sts in moss st, 4 sts in feather faggot st, 2 sts in moss st, YO, P2tog, 21 (24, 28, 31) sts in moss st, K1.

Row 105 (111, 115, 121): K1, work 16 (19, 23, 26) sts in moss st, YO, P2tog, 3 sts in moss st, YO, P2tog, 2 sts in moss st, K1, YO, P2tog, K1, 2 sts in moss st, YO, P2tog, 3 sts in moss st, YO, P2tog, 16 (19, 23, 26) sts in moss st, K1.

Row 111 (117, 121, 127): K1, work 11 (14, 18, 21) sts in moss st, (YO, P2tog, 3 sts in moss st) twice, YO, P2tog, 2 sts in moss st, K1, YO, P2tog, K1, 2 sts in moss st, (YO, P2tog, 3 sts in moss st) twice, YO, P2tog, 11 (14, 18, 21) sts in moss st, K1.

Row 117 (123, 127, 133): K1, work 6 (9, 13, 16) sts in moss st, (YO, P2tog, 3 sts in moss st) 3 times, YO, P2tog, 2 sts in moss st, K1, YO, P2tog, K1, 2 sts in moss st, (YO, P2tog, 3 sts in moss st) 3 times, YO, P2tog, 6 (9, 13, 16) sts in moss st, K1.

Cont in est patt through row 125 (131, 135, 141).

Shape neck:

Row 126 (132, 136, 142): Work 15 (16, 19, 21) sts in patt, BO 26 (30, 32, 34) center sts, work in patt to end.

Attach second ball of yarn to second st at beg of neck edge, dec 1 st, and then BO 1 st at neck edge on next 4 rows. For final neck dec, row 131 (137, 141, 147): dec 1 st at each neck edge, work 8 (9, 12, 14) sts in patt, then K2tog and for other side K2tog tbl, then work 8 (9, 12, 14) sts in patt. Work 3 rows even. Mark row 133 (139, 143, 149) with a safety pin to indicate center of neck and where a shoulder seam would be if shell were not worked in one piece. After this row, move into back of shell.

Row 135 (141, 145, 151): Inc 1 st at each neck edge using K1f&b in edge st. On next 2 rows, at beg of neck edge, use knitted CO to inc 2 sts. On next 2 rows, at beg of neck edge, use knitted CO to inc 3 sts. After CO row, work sts in patt to correspond to front.

Row 140 (146, 150, 156): Work 15 (16, 19, 21) sts in patt and use knitted CO to inc 26 (30, 32, 34) center neck sts, then join to other side shoulder sts and work in patt to end. Cont to work all patts as for front, feather faggot stripes will cont on back all the way to moss bottom edging rather than being utilized only as upper body accent on front. Work even for another 37 (39, 41, 43) rows.

Shape armholes: At beg of next 2 rows, use knitted CO to inc 1 (2, 2, 3) st through rows 178–179 (186–187, 192–193, 200–201). At beg of next 2 rows, use knitted CO to inc 3 (3, 4, 4) sts—64 (72, 82, 90) sts. Work 17 (19, 19, 21) rows even through row 198 (208, 214, 224).

Shape waist:

Row 199 (209, 215, 225): Dec 1 st at each edge inside selvage sts.

Rep dec every 6 rows 3 times.

Work 5 rows even.

Row 223 (233, 239, 249): Inc 1 st each edge using M1.

Rep inc every 6 rows 3 times.

Work 12 (14, 16, 18) rows even.

Work 11 rows in moss st. BO in patt on next row.

finishing

Meticulously block to measurements.

Sew side seams using invisible vertical seaming.

Armhole finishing: With RS facing you and using circular needle, beg at underarm seam and PU 80 (82, 84, 86) sts. Work 1 rnd in K1, P1 ribbing, and BO in patt on next rnd.

Neck finishing: Using circular needle, PU 94 (98, 102, 106) sts and work as for armholes.

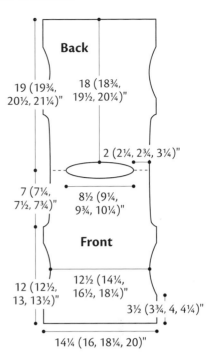

Back

19 (19¾, 20½, 21¼)" 18 (18¾, 19½, 20¼)"

2 (2¼, 2¾, 3¼)"

7 (7¼, 7½, 7¾)" 8½ (9¼, 9¾, 10¼)"

Front

12 (12½, 13, 13½)" 12½ (14¼, 16½, 18¼)"

3½ (3¾, 4, 4¼)"

14¼ (16, 18¼, 20)"

seed and triple gull cable CARDIGAN and SKIRT

Wrap yourself in the luxury, comfort, and warmth of this soft-as-can-be baby alpaca sweater and skirt. Softness prevails in the graceful and elegant lines of the skirt that are enhanced by its gored shape and in the shawl-like collar of the cardigan.

Skill Level: Intermediate ◼◼◼▢

Size: Small (Medium, Large, Extra Large)

Finished Measurements

Cardigan Bust: 36½ (39, 44½, 47)"

Cardigan Length: 21½ (22½, 23½, 24½)"

Skirt Waist: 27 (29½, 32, 34½)"

Skirt Length: 25¾"

MATERIALS

Misti Alpaca from Misti International (100% baby alpaca; 50 g; 146 yds) in color NT-408 ▨**2**

  Cardigan: 8 (9, 10, 11) skeins

  Skirt: 8 (9, 10, 11) skeins

Size 5 (3.75 mm) needles or size required to obtain gauge

Cable needle

11½ (12, 12½, 13)" of grosgrain ribbon to match yarn for buttonhole facing

Thread in matching color for sewing ribbon and buttons

6 to 8 buttons, ⅝" diameter (cardigan is shown with brown mother-of-pearl buttons)

1 yd of nonroll, ¾"-wide elastic for skirt

GAUGE

24 sts and 40 rows = 4" in triple gull and seed st patts when blocked

PATTERN STITCHES

4-St Triple Gull Cable

See chart on page 43.

(Multiple of 4 sts)

Rows 1, 9, and 11 (RS): K4.

Rows 2, 4, and 6: P1, sl 2 wyif, P1.

Rows 3, 5, and 7: Sl 1 st to cn and hold in back, K1, K1 from cn, sl next st to cn and hold in front, K1, K1 from cn.

Rows 8, 10, and 12: P4.

Rep rows 1–12 for patt.

6-St Triple Gull Cable

See chart on page 43.

(Multiple of 6 sts)

Rows 1, 9, and 11 (RS): K6.

Rows 2, 4, and 6: P2, sl 2 wyif, P2.

Rows 3, 5, and 7: Sl 2 sts to cn and hold in back, K1, K2 from cn, sl next st to cn and hold in front, K2, K1 from cn.

Rows 8, 10, and 12: P6.

Rep rows 1–12 for patt.

Seed Stitch

(Over an even number of sts)

Row 1: *K1, P1; rep from *.

Row 2: *P1, K1; rep from *.

Rep rows 1 and 2 for patt.

SELVAGE STITCHES

Selvage stitches are identified in parentheses in the first two rows of the pattern and are included in the instructions for the following rows without being labeled as such.

CARDIGAN INSTRUCTIONS

back

Cable CO 110 (118, 134, 142) sts.

Row 1 (RS): K1 (selvage st), P1, *K2, P2; rep from * to last 4 sts, K2, P1, K1 (selvage st).

Row 2: K1 (selvage st), K1, *P2, K2; rep from * to last 4 sts, P2, K1, K1 (selvage st).

Rows 3 and 4: Rep rows 1 and 2.

Row 5: Rep row 1.

Rows 6, 7, 11, and 12: Knit.

Rows 8, 9, and 10: K1, purl to last st, K1.

Work first patt section using 4-st triple gull cable.

Row 13: K1, *(K1, P1) twice, work 4-st triple gull cable (row 1); rep from * to last 5 sts, (K1, P1) twice, K1.

Row 14: K1, *(P1, K1) twice, work 4-st triple gull cable (row 2); rep from * to last 5 sts, (P1, K1) twice, K1.

Row 15: K1, *(K1, P1) twice, work 4-st triple gull cable (row 3); rep from * to last 5 sts, (K1, P1) twice, K1.

Rows 16–19: Rep rows 14 and 15.

Row 20: K1, *(P1, K1) twice, work 4-st triple gull cable (row 8); rep from * to last 5 sts, (P1, K1) twice, K1.

Rows 21–25: Rep rows 13 and 20.

Rows 26–31: Rep rows 14 and 15.

Rows 32, 33, 37, and 38: Knit.

Rows 34–36: K1, purl to last st, K1.

Work next patt section using 6-st triple gull cable.

Row 39: (K1, P1) 5 (4, 5, 4) times, *work 6-st triple gull cable (row 1), (K1, P1) 3 times; rep from * to last 16 (14, 16, 14) sts, work 6-st triple gull cable, (K1, P1) 4 (3, 4, 3) times, K2.

Row 40: K2, (P1, K1) 4 (3, 4, 3) times, *work 6-st triple gull cable (row 2), (P1, K1) 3 times; rep from * to last 16 (14, 16, 14) sts, work 6-st triple gull cable, (P1, K1) 5 (4, 5, 4) times.

Cont in est patt until work measures 13½ (14, 14½, 15)" from beg, or approx through row 134 (140, 144, 150).

Shape armholes: BO 4 (4, 5, 6) sts at beg of next 2 rows. Dec 1 st, then BO 1 (2, 2, 2) st at beg of next 2 rows—98 (104, 118, 124) sts. Work even until armhole is 7½ (8, 8½, 9)".

Shape shoulders: BO 8 (9, 10, 11) sts at beg of next 2 rows. Dec 1 st, then BO 8 (9, 10, 11) sts at beg of next 2 rows. Dec 1 st, then BO 9 (9, 11, 11) sts at beg of next 2 rows. BO rem 44 (46, 52, 54) sts on next row. Note that you will omit sl 2 of row 2 triple gull cable and work as P2 if it occurs in last WS row before neck BO, and omit cable crossing of row 3 triple gull cable if it occurs in last RS row that is BO row.

fronts

With separate balls of yarn, cable CO 52 (56, 64, 68) sts for right and left front at same time. Directions are written for right side of front and must be reversed for left side.

Row 1 (RS): K1 (selvage st), *P2, K2; rep from * to last 3 sts, P2, K1 (selvage st).

Row 2: K1, *K2, P2; rep from * to last 3 sts, K2, K1.

Rows 3–12: Work as for back.

Work first patt section using 4-st triple gull cable.

Row 13: K1, (K1, P1) 1 (2, 2, 1) time, *work 4-st triple gull cable (row 1), (K1, P1) twice; rep from * to last 1 (3, 3, 1) st, (K1, P1) 0 (1, 1, 0) times, K1.

Row 14: K1, (P1, K1) 0 (1, 1, 0) times, *(P1, K1) twice, work 4-st triple gull cable (row 2); rep from * to last 3 (5, 5, 3) sts, (P1, K1) 1 (2, 2, 1) time, K1.

Row 15: K1, (K1, P1) 1 (2, 2, 1) time, *work 4-st triple gull cable (row 3), (K1, P1) twice; rep from * to last 1 (3, 3, 1) st, (K1, P1) 0 (1, 1, 0) times, K1.

Rows 16–19: Rep rows 14 and 15.

Row 20: K1, (P1, K1) 0 (1, 1, 0) times, *(P1, K1) twice, work 4-st triple gull cable (row 8); rep from * to last 3 (5, 5, 3) sts, (P1, K1) 1 (2, 2, 1) time, K1.

Rows 21–25: Rep rows 13 and 20.

Rows 26–31: Rep rows 14 and 15.

Rows 32, 33, 37, and 38: Knit.

Rows 34–36: K1, purl to last st, K1.

Work next patt section using 6-st triple gull cable.

Row 39: (K1, P1) 1 (2, 1, 2) time, *work 6-st triple gull cable (row 1), (K1, P1) 3 times; rep from * to last 2 (4, 2, 4) sts, (K1, P1) 0 (1, 0, 1) times, K2.

Row 40: K1, P1, (P1, K1) 0 (1, 0, 1) times, *(P1, K1) 3 times, work 6-st triple gull cable (row 2); rep from * to last 2 (4, 2, 4) sts, (P1, K1) 1 (2, 1, 2) time.

Cont in est patt until work measures 11 (11½, 12, 12½)" from beg, or approx through row 110 (115, 120, 125).

Shape neck: Dec 1 st at neck edge EOR 2 (2, 3, 4) times, every 4 rows 2 (3, 5, 5) times and every 6 rows 15 times. Note that neck shaping for right front occurs on RS rows and for left front on WS rows. AT SAME TIME shape armholes and shoulders as for back.

sleeves

Cable CO 48 (52, 52, 56) sts. Work rows 1–12 as for front and on row 12, inc 1 (0, 1, 0) st at each edge inside selvage sts—50 (52, 54, 56) sts.

Work first patt section using 4-st triple gull cable.

Row 13: K1 (selvage st), P0 (0, 0, 1), K0 (0, 1, 1), P0 (1, 1, 1), K1, P1, *work 4-st triple gull cable (row 1), (K1, P1) twice; rep from * to last 7 (8, 9, 10) sts, work 4-st triple gull cable (row 1), K1, P1, K0 (1, 1, 1), P0 (0, 1, 1), K0 (0, 0, 1), K1 (selvage st).

Row 14: K1, K0 (0, 0, 1), P0 (0, 1, 1), K0 (1, 1, 1), P1, K1, *work 4-st triple gull cable (row 2), (P1, K1) twice; rep from * to last 7 (8, 9, 10) sts, work 4-st triple gull cable (row 2), P1, K1, P0 (1, 1, 1), K0 (0, 1, 1), P0 (0, 0, 1), K1.

Row 15: K1, P0 (0, 0, 1), K0 (0, 1, 1), P0 (1, 1, 1), K1, P1, *work 4-st triple gull cable (row 3), (K1, P1) twice; rep from * to last 7 (8, 9, 10) sts, work 4-st triple gull cable, K1, P1, K0 (1, 1, 1), P0 (0, 1, 1), K0 (0, 0, 1), K1.

Rows 16–19: Rep rows 14 and 15.

Row 20: K1, K0 (0, 0, 1), P0 (0, 1, 1), K0 (1, 1, 1), P1, K1, *work 4-st triple gull cable (row 8), (P1, K1) twice; rep from * to last 7 (8, 9, 10) sts, work 4-st triple gull cable (row 8), P1, K1, P0 (1, 1, 1), K0 (0, 1, 1), P0 (0, 0, 1), K1.

Rows 21–25: Rep rows 13 and 20. Beg sleeve shaping on row 24, see next line.

Shape sleeves: Beg row 24, inc 1 st at each edge inside selvage st. Beg row 32, work this inc every 8 rows 17 (17,18, 19) more times, working all incs in seed st to 86 (88, 92, 96) total sts.

Rows 26–31: Rep rows 14 and 15.

Rows 32, 33, 37, and 38: Knit.

Rows 34–36: K1, purl to last st, K1.

Work next patt section using 6-st triple gull cable.

Row 39: K0 (1, 1, 1), K0 (0, 1, 1), P0 (0, 0, 1), *work 6-st triple gull cable (row 1), 6 sts in seed stitch as (K1, P1) 3 times; rep from * to last 6 (7, 8, 9) sts, work 6-st triple gull cable, K0 (0, 0, 1), P0 (0, 1, 1), K0 (1, 1, 1)—54 (56, 58, 60) sts.

Cont in est patt until work measures 16 1/2 (17, 17 1/2, 18)" from beg, or approx through row 165 (170, 175. 180).

Shape caps: BO 4 (4, 5, 6) sts at beg of next 2 rows. Dec 1 st, then BO 1 (2, 2, 2) st at beg of next 2 rows—74 (74, 76, 78) sts. Dec 1 st at beg of next 26 (30, 34, 36) rows. Dec 1 st at each edge on next 10 (8, 7, 7) rows. Dec 1 st, then BO 1 st at beg of next 2 rows. Dec 1 st, then BO 2 sts at beg of next 2 rows. BO rem 18 sts on next row.

collar

Cable CO 180 (188, 204, 212) sts. Work rows 1–12 as for front.

Work main patt using 4-st triple gull cable.

Row 13: (K1, P1) twice, *work 4-st triple gull cable (row 1), (K1, P1) twice, rep from * to end.

Row 14: (P1, K1) twice, *work 4-st triple gull cable (row 2), (P1, K1) twice; rep from *.

Row 15: (K1, P1) twice, *work 4-st triple gull cable (row 3), (K1, P1) twice; rep from *.

Rows 16–19: Rep rows 14 and 15.

Row 20: (P1, K1) twice, *work 4-st triple gull cable (row 8), (P1, K1) twice; rep from *.

Rows 21–26: Rep rows 13 and 20.

Rows 27–30: Rep rows 15 and 16.

Row 31: Rep row 15.

Rows 32, 33, 37, 38, and 39: Knit.

Rows 34–36: K1, purl to last st, K1.

Row 40: BO all sts pw.

Note that rows 39 and 40 create an edge to sew the collar in place.

finishing

Block all pieces to measurements.

Sew shoulder seams using invisible horizontal seaming, referring to "Joining Textured Shoulders" on page 12.

Button band (left side): With RS facing you, PU 66 (70, 72, 74) sts from left to right. Work as follows.

Rows 1–7: Work in seed st.

Row 8: Knit. Note that this row will be fold line.

Rows 9–15: Work in St st, beg and end with knit row and BO on last row. Note that these rows will become facing for button-band edging.

Buttonhole band (right side): With RS facing you, PU 66 (70, 72, 74) sts from left to right and work as follows.

Rows 1, 2, and 3: Work in seed st.

Row 4 (WS): Work 2 (3, 4, 3) sts, *work 1 row horizontal buttonhole, work 9 (9, 9, 10) sts; rep from * 3 times, work 1 row horizontal buttonhole, work 8 (10, 10, 10) sts, work 1 row horizontal buttonhole, work 2 (3, 4, 3) sts. Note that 1 row horizontal buttonhole equals BO 3 sts and cable CO 4 sts. (See page 75.)

Rows 5, 6, and 7: Work in seed st.

Row 8: BO all sts kw. Note that this edge is faced with matching grosgrain ribbon.

BUTTONHOLE TIP

I had a seamstress work buttonholes in the ribbon corresponding with buttonholes in the knit edge for a very small fee.

Finishing front bands: Steam block button bands. Sew buttons in place to correspond with buttonholes. Seam St st facing in place using whipstitch. Whipstitch grosgrain ribbon with machined buttonholes in place to correspond with knit button-holes. Whipstitch ends of bands closed.

Set in sleeves using invisible vertical to horizontal seaming.

Sew side and underarm seams using invisible vertical seaming.

Pin collar in place beg at center back of neck with RS of collar against WS of sweater. Collar will not be attached to top edge of button bands. Pin evenly between initial pinning. Whipstitch edges of neck and collar tog, sewing through both loops of BO edge of collar.

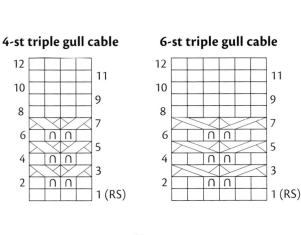

4-st triple gull cable   **6-st triple gull cable**

Key

☐	K on RS, P on WS
∩	Sl 1 wyif
	Sl 1 st to cn and hold in back, K1, K1 from cn
	Sl 1 st to cn and hold in front, K1, K1 from cn
	Sl 2 sts to cn and hold in back, K1, K2 from cn
	Sl 1 st to cn and hold in front, K2, K1 from cn

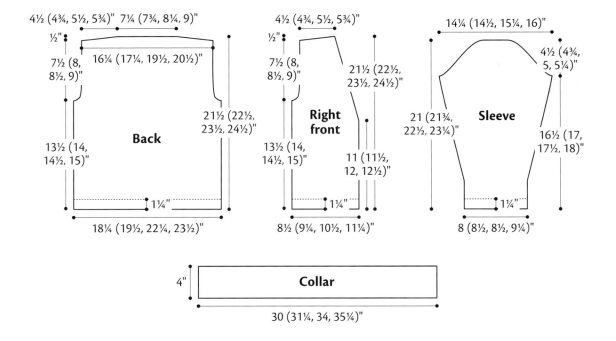

Back: 4½ (4¾, 5½, 5¾)" 7¼ (7¾, 8¼, 9)" ½" 7½ (8, 8½, 9)" 16¼ (17¼, 19½, 20½)" 21½ (22½, 23½, 24½)" 13½ (14, 14½, 15)" 1¼" 18¼ (19½, 22¼, 23½)"

Right front: 4½ (4¾, 5½, 5¾)" ½" 7½ (8, 8½, 9)" 21½ (22½, 23½, 24½)" 13½ (14, 14½, 15)" 11 (11½, 12, 12½)" 1¼" 8½ (9¼, 10½, 11¼)"

Sleeve: 14¼ (14½, 15¼, 16)" 4½ (4¾, 5, 5¼)" 21 (21¾, 22½, 23¼)" 16½ (17, 17½, 18)" 1¼" 8 (8½, 8½, 9¼)"

Collar: 4" 30 (31¼, 34, 35¼)"

SKIRT INSTRUCTIONS

front and back

Make 2 pieces the same.

Using size 5 needles, cable CO 180 (188, 196, 204) sts.

Rows 1, 3, and 5: K1 (selvage st), *K2, P2, rep from * to last 3 sts, K2, K1 (selvage st).

Rows 2 and 4: K1 (selvage st), *P2, K2, rep from * to last 3 sts, P2, K1 (selvage st).

Row 6: Knit.

Work first patt section using 6-st triple gull cable.

Row 7: K1, (K1, P1) 3 (5, 3, 5) times, *work 6-st triple gull cable (row 1), (K1, P1) 7 (7, 8, 8) times; rep from * to last 13 (17, 13, 17) sts, work 6-st triple gull cable (row 1), (K1, P1) 3 (5, 3, 5) times, K1.

Cont in patt as est through row 36.

Shape bottom of skirt: Cont in est patt, working decs on following rows.

Row 37: K1, (K1, P1) 2 (4, 2, 4) times, K2tog tbl, work 6-st triple gull cable (row 7), *P2tog, (K1, P1) 5 (5, 6, 6) times, K2tog tbl, work 6-st triple gull cable, rep from * to last 7 (11, 7, 11) sts, P2tog, (K1, P1) 2 (4, 2, 4) times, K1—162 (170, 178, 186) sts.

Row 49: K1 (K1, P1) 1 (3, 1, 3) time, K1, P2tog tbl, work 6-st triple gull cable (row 7), *K2tog, (P1, K1) 4 (4, 5, 5) times, P2tog tbl, work 6-st triple gull cable, rep from * to last 6 (10, 6, 10) sts, K2tog, (P1, K1) 2 (4, 2, 4) times.

Row 61: K1 (K1, P1) 1 (3, 1, 3) time, K2tog tbl, work 6-st triple gull cable (row 7), *P2tog, (K1, P1) 3 (3, 4, 4) times, K2tog tbl, work 6-st triple gull cable, rep from * to last 5 (9, 5, 9) sts, P2tog, (K1, P1) 1 (3, 1, 3) time, K1.

Row 73

Small (Large): K2, P2tog tbl, work 6-st triple gull cable (row 7), *K2tog, (P1, K1) 2 (3) times, P2tog tbl, work 6-st triple gull cable; rep from * to last 4 sts, K2tog, (P1, K1)—108 (124) sts.

Medium (Extra Large): K1, (P1, K1) twice, P1, K2tog tbl, work 6-st triple gull cable (row 7), *K2tog, (P1, K1) 2 (3) times, P2tog tbl, work 6-st triple gull cable; rep from * to last 8 sts, K2tog, (P1, K1) 3 times—116 (132) sts.

Rows 74 and 75: Work in est patt.

Rows 76 and 77: Knit.

Rows 78, 79, and 80: K1, purl to last st, K1.

Rows 81 and 82: Knit.

Row 83: *(K1, P1) twice, work 4-st triple gull cable (row 1); rep from * to last 4 sts, (K1, P1) twice.

Row 84: *(P1, K1) twice, work 4-st triple gull cable (row 2); rep from * to last 4 sts, (P1, K1) twice.

Row 85: *(K1, P1) twice, work 4-st triple gull cable (row 3); rep from * to last 4 sts, (K1, P1) twice.

Cont in est patt through row 101.

Rows 102, 103, 107, and 108: Knit.

Rows 104–106: K1, purl to last st, K1.

Row 109: K1, (K1, P1) 1 (3, 1, 3) time, work 6-st triple gull cable (row 1), *(K1, P1) 3 (3, 4, 4) times, work 6-st triple gull cable, rep from * to last 3 (7, 3, 7) sts, (K1, P1) 1 (3, 1, 3) time, K1.

Row 110: K1, (P1, K1) 1 (3, 1, 3) time, work 6-st triple gull cable (row 2), *(P1, K1) 3 (3, 4, 4) times, work 6-st triple gull cable; rep from * to last 3 (7, 3, 7) sts, (P1, K1) 1 (3, 1, 3) time, K1.

Cont in patt as est until work measures 18" from beg, approx 180 rows total.

Shape from hips to waist: Dec 1 st at each edge every 8 rows 4 times; every 6 rows 4 times; every 4 rows 4 times, and EOR twice—80 (88, 96, 104) sts.

Work waistband:

Row 250: Knit.

Row 251: K1, *P2, K2, rep from * to last 3 sts, P2, K1.

Row 252: K3, *P2, K2, rep from * to last 5 sts, P2, K3.

Rows 253–256: Rep rows 251 and 252.

Row 257: Rep row 251.

Row 258: Knit. This creates fold line for waistband.

Rows 259–264: Work in St st.

BO all sts kw on next row.

finishing

Steam block front and back to measurements.

Sew side seams using invisible vertical seaming.

Fold waistband and whipstitch into place on inside of garment, leaving a 1" to 2" opening. Attach a safety pin to end of waist elastic and work through waistband. Remove safety pin. Seam edges of elastic. Finish closing remainder of waistband.

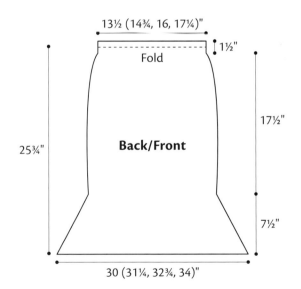

13½ (14¾, 16, 17¼)"

Fold

1½"

17½"

Back/Front

25¾"

7½"

30 (31¼, 32¾, 34)"

uneven cable TURTLENECK, HEADBAND, and VEST

Skill Level: Intermediate ■■■◻

Turtleneck and Vest Size: Small (Medium, Large, Extra Large)

Finished Measurements

Turtleneck Bust: 35 (39½, 43½, 48)"

Turtleneck Length: 20 (21, 22, 23)"

Headband Circumference: Knit to fit

Vest Bust: 37½ (41, 45½, 49)"

Vest Length: 21½ (22½, 23½, 24½)"

MATERIALS FOR TURTLENECK AND HEADBAND

Nature Spun Sportweight from Brown Sheep Company (100% wool; 1.75 oz/50 g; 184 yds/168 m) in color 740 Snow

Turtleneck: 8 (9, 10, 11) skeins

Headband: one quarter of a skein

Size 4 (3.5 mm) and 5 (3.75 mm) needles or size required to obtain gauge

Size 4 (3.5 mm) circular needle (16") for turtleneck

Cable needle

MATERIALS FOR VEST

5 (5, 6, 7) skeins of Lamb's Pride Worsted from Brown Sheep Company (85% wool, 15% mohair; 4 oz/113 g; 190 yds/173 m) in color M-11 White Frost ④

Size 7 (4.5 mm) and 8 (5 mm) needles or size required to obtain gauge

Size 7 (4.5 mm) circular needle (16") for neck edging

Cable needle

1 toggle button, 1½" long

GAUGE

Turtleneck and headband: 30 sts and 32 rows = 4" in combination of st patts on larger needles

Vest: 20 sts and 28 rows = 4" in combination of st patts on larger needles.

PATTERN STITCHES

Uneven 6-Stitch Cable

See chart on page 50.

(Multiple of 6 sts)

UC6B (uneven cable 6 back): sl next 2 sts to cn and hold in back, K4, K2 from cn.

UC6F (uneven cable 6 front): sl next 4 sts to cn and hold in front, K2, K4 from cn.

Rows 1 and 5 (RS): K6.

Rows 2 and 4: P6.

Row 3: UC6B or UC6F (as indicated).

Row 6: P6.

Rep rows 1–6 for patt.

Uneven 3-Stitch Cable

See chart on page 50.

(Multiple of 3 sts)

UC3B (uneven cable 3 back): sl next st to cn and hold in back, K2, K1 from cn.

UC3F (uneven cable 3 front): sl next 2 sts to cn and hold in front, K1, K2 from cn.

Row 1 (RS): K3.

Row 2: P3.

Row 3: UC3B or UC3F (as indicated).

Row 4: P3.

Rep rows 1–4 for patt.

These are versatile and high-impact pieces, with their unusual uneven cable and interesting use of vertical and horizontal ribs, that you'll wear again and again. The turtleneck delights in its saddle-back shoulder that continues into the neck. The vest with its shawl collar goes with everything. Use the headband to keep your ears warm and happy.

Right Twist (RT): K2tog leaving sts on left needle, insert right needle between 2 sts just knit tog, and knit through front of first st again, then sl both sts from needle tog.

Left Twist (LT): With right-hand needle behind left-hand needle, sk 1 st and knit the second st tbl, then insert right-hand needle into the back of both sts (skipped st and second st) and K2tog tbl.

SELVAGE STITCHES

Selvage stitches are identified in parentheses in the first two rows of the pattern and are included in the instructions for the following rows without being labeled as such.

TURTLENECK INSTRUCTIONS

front

With smaller needles, cable CO 132 (148, 164, 180) sts and work bottom ribbing as follows.

Row 1 (RS): K1 (selvage st), *P2, K2; rep from * to last 3 sts, P2, K1 (selvage st).

Row 2: K1 (selvage st), *K2, P2; rep from * to last 3 sts, K2, K1 (selvage st).

Rep rows 1 and 2 for a total of 13 rows.

Row 14: K1, purl to last st, K1.

Change to larger needles and est main patts as follows.

Row 1 (RS)

Small: K1, P1, (P2, K2) 2 times, P2, RT, P2, K3, P2, RT, (P2, K3, P2, RT, P2, K6, P2, RT) 2 times, P2, (LT, P2,

K6, P2, LT, P2, K3, P2) 2 times, LT, P2, K3, P2, LT, P2, (K2, P2) 2 times, P1, K1.

Medium: K1, P1, (P2, K2) 4 times, P2, RT, P2, K3, P2, RT, (P2, K3, P2, RT, P2, K6, P2, RT) 2 times, P2, (LT, P2, K6, P2, LT, P2, K3, P2) 2 times, LT, P2, K3, P2, LT, P2, (K2, P2) 4 times, P1, K1.

Large: K1, (P2, K2) 3 times, (P2, RT, P2, K3, P2, RT) 2 times, (P2, K3, P2, RT, P2, K6, P2, RT) 2 times, P2, (LT, P2, K6, P2, LT, P2, K3, P2) 2 times, (LT, P2, K3, P2, LT, P2) 2 times, (K2, P2) 3 times, K1.

Extra Large: K1, (P2, K2) 3 times, P2, RT, P2, K3, P2, RT, (P2, K3, P2, RT, P2, K6, P2, RT) 3 times, P2, (LT, P2, K6, P2, LT, P2, K3, P2) 3 times, LT, P2, K3, P2, LT, P2, (K2, P2) 3 times, K1.

Row 2 (WS)

Small: K2, (K2, P2) 2 times, K2, P2, K2, P3, K2, P2, (K2, P3, K2, P2, K2, P6, K2, P2) 2 times, K2, (P2, K2, P6, K2, P2, K2, P3, K2) 2 times, P2, K2, P3, K2, P2, K2, (P2, K2) 2 times, K2.

Medium: K2, (K2, P2) 4 times, K2, P2, K2, P3, K2, P2, (K2, P3, K2, P2, K2, P6, K2, P2) 2 times, K2, (P2, K2, P6, K2, P2, K2, P3, K2) 2 times, P2, K2, P3, K2, P2, K2, (P2, K2) 4 times, K2.

Large: K1, (K2, P2) 3 times, (K2, P2, K2, P3, K2, P2) 2 times, (K2, P3, K2, P2, K2, P6, K2, P2) 2 times, K2, (P2, K2, P6, K2, P2, K2, P3, K2) 2 times, (P2, K2, P3, K2, P2, K2) 2 times, (P2, K2) 3 times, K1.

Extra Large: K1, (K2, P2) 3 times, K2, P2, K2, P3, K2, P2, (K2, P3, K2, P2, K2, P6, K2, P2) 3 times, K2, (P2, K2, P6, K2, P2, K2, P3, K2) 3 times, P2, K2, P3, K2, P2, K2, (P2, K2) 3 times, K1.

Row 3 (RS)

Small: K1, P1, (P2, K2) 2 times, P2, RT, P2, UC3B, P2, RT, (P2, UC3B, P2, RT, P2, UC6B, P2, RT) 2 times, P2, (LT, P2, UC6F, P2, LT, P2, UC3F, P2) 2 times, LT, P2, UC3F, P2, LT, P2, (K2, P2) 2 times, P1, K1.

Medium: K1, P1, (P2, K2) 4 times, P2, RT, P2, UC3B, P2, RT, (P2, UC3B, P2, RT, P2, UC6B, P2, RT) 2 times, P2, (LT, P2, UC6F, P2, LT, P2, UC3F, P2) 2 times, LT, P2, UC3F, P2, LT, P2, (K2, P2) 4 times, P1, K1.

Large: K1, (P2, K2) 3 times, (P2, RT, P2, UC3B, P2, RT) 2 times, (P2, UC3B, P2, RT, P2, UC6B, P2, RT) 2 times, P2, (LT, P2, UC6F, P2, LT, P2, UC3F, P2) 2 times, (LT, P2, UC3F, P2, LT, P2) 2 times, (K2, P2) 3 times, K1.

Extra Large: K1, (P2, K2) 3 times, P2, RT, P2, UC3B, P2, RT, (P2, UC3B, P2, RT, P2, UC6B, P2, RT) 3 times, P2, (LT, P2, UC6F, P2, LT, P2, UC3F, P2) 3 times, LT, P2, UC3F, P2, LT, P2, (K2, P2) 3 times, K1.

Remember that the 3-st uneven cable crosses every 4 rows and the 6-st uneven cable crosses every 6 rows.

Cont in patt until front measures 13½ (14, 14½, 15)" from beg, approx through row 94 (98, 102, 106) of main patt, plus 14 rows of ribbing.

Shape armholes: BO 5 (6, 7, 7) sts at beg of next 2 rows. Dec 1 st, then BO 2 (2, 2, 3) sts at beg of next 2 rows. Dec 1 st at beg of next 2 rows—114 (128, 142, 156) sts rem.

Cont in patt until front measures 19 (20, 21, 22)" from beg, approx through row 138 (146, 154, 162) of main patt, plus 14 rows of ribbing.

Shape shoulders and neck: BO 8 (9, 10, 11) sts at beg of next 2 rows to beg shoulder shaping. Next row: Dec 1 st, then BO 7 (8, 10, 11) sts at shoulder edge and in same row beg neck shaping with BO of 26 (28, 30, 32) center sts, and finish row. Work both sides at same time. With 1 ball of yarn, dec 1 st, then BO 7 (8, 10, 11) sts at shoulder edge, and attach second ball of yarn to second neck st, dec 1 st, then BO 5 (6, 7, 8) sts at beg of neck edge of same row. Cont in this manner with 2 balls of yarn. On next row, dec 1 st, then BO 8 (9, 10, 11) sts at shoulder edge and dec 1 st, then BO 5 (6, 7, 8) sts at beg of neck edge. On next row, dec 1 st, then BO 8 (9, 10, 11) sts at shoulder edge, and dec 1 st, then BO 2 (3, 3, 4) sts at beg of neck edge. On next row, dec 1 st, then BO 9 (10, 11, 12) sts at shoulder edge and dec 1 st, then BO 2 (3, 3, 4) sts at beg of neck edge. On final row, dec 1 st, then BO 9 (10, 11, 12) sts at shoulder edge.

back

Work as for front without working any neck shaping. After final shoulder dec, place rem 44 (50, 54, 60) sts at back of neck on st holder or use separate strand of yarn to hold these sts.

sleeves

With larger needles, cable CO 68 (68, 72, 72) sts for each sleeve with separate balls of yarn.

Row 1 (RS)

Left sleeve: (K2, P2) 6 (6, 7, 7) times, RT, (P2, K3, P2, RT) twice, (P2, K2) 6 (6, 7, 7) times.

Right sleeve: Work as above working all RT as LT.

Row 2 (WS)

Both sleeves for all WS rows: K1 (selvage st), purl the purl sts and knit the knit sts as they face you to last st, K1 (selvage st).

Row 3: Rep row 1, working K3 as UC3B on left sleeve and UC3F on right sleeve.

Cont in est patt, crossing the cable as est on every fourth row.

Shape sleeves: On row 11, inc 1 st at each edge as follows: K1, M1, cont in patt to last st, M1, K1. Work M1 inc kw or pw as needed to maintain ribbing patt. Work incs at each edge every 6 rows 19 (20, 8, 13) times, and every 8 rows 0 (0, 9, 6) times—108 (110, 112, 116) sts, approx through row 132 (136, 140, 144), and 16½ (17, 17½, 18)" from beg.

Shape caps: BO 5 (6, 7, 7) sts at beg of next 2 rows. Dec 1 st, then BO 2 (2, 2, 3) sts at beg of next 2 rows. Dec 1 st at beg of next 2 (4, 6, 8) rows. Dec 1 st at each edge of next 25 rows. Dec 1 st, then BO 1 st at beg of next 2 rows. Dec 1 st, then BO 2 (2, 1, 1) sts at beg of next 2 rows. Dec 1 st, then BO 3 (2, 2, 2) sts at beg of next 2 rows—22 sts rem.

Saddles: Work even for 37 (41, 45, 51) rows, approx 4¾". Next 2 rows: for right sleeve on RS row, BO kw 11 sts; for left sleeve on WS row, BO pw 11 sts. Last 2 rows: for right sleeve on RS row, dec 1 st, BO kw 10 sts; for left sleeve on WS row, dec 1 st, BO pw 10 sts.

finishing

Meticulously block to measurements.

Seam saddleback shoulder strips to front and back using invisible vertical to horizontal seaming.

Seam sleeves to armholes using invisible vertical to horizontal seaming.

Seam sides and underarm sleeve seams using invisible vertical seaming.

Turtleneck: Using circular needle, place 44 (50, 54, 60) back-neck sts on needle, PU 1 (0, 1, 1) st between back of neck and saddleback shoulder, PU 20 sts over right saddleback shoulder, PU 46 (50, 56, 62) front neck sts, PU 20 sts over left saddleback shoulder, PU 1 (0, 1, 1) st between saddleback shoulder and back of neck—132 (140, 152, 164) sts.

Rnd 1: P1, working above left saddleback shoulder, matching patt in shoulder leading into neck with same patt as follows, RT, (P2, K3, P2, RT) twice, P2, (K2, P2) 11 (12, 14, 15) times, working above right saddleback shoulder LT, (P2, K3, P2, LT) twice, (P2, K2) 11 (12, 14, 15) times, P1.

Rnds 2 and 4: Knit the knit sts and purl the purl sts as they face you.

Rnd 3: Rep row 1, working row 3 of uneven cable cross for all K3 and crossing the cables as indicated from saddleback shoulder.

Rep rnds 1–4 through row 27. BO all sts in patt on next row.

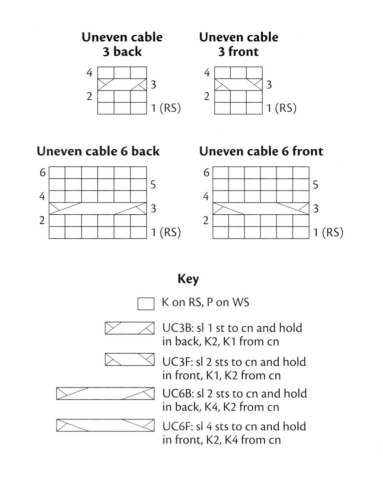

Uneven cable 3 back

Uneven cable 3 front

Uneven cable 6 back

Uneven cable 6 front

Key

☐ K on RS, P on WS

⬓ UC3B: sl 1 st to cn and hold in back, K2, K1 from cn

⬓ UC3F: sl 2 sts to cn and hold in front, K1, K2 from cn

⬓ UC6B: sl 2 sts to cn and hold in back, K4, K2 from cn

⬓ UC6F: sl 4 sts to cn and hold in front, K2, K4 from cn

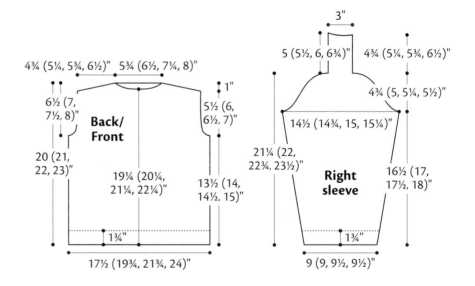

HEADBAND INSTRUCTIONS

With smaller needles, cable CO 16 sts.

Row 1 (RS): K1 (selvage st), *P2, K2, rep from * to last 3 sts, P2, K1 (selvage st).

Row 2 (WS): K1 (selvage st), *K2, P2, rep from * to last 3 sts, K3.

Rep these 2 rows until work measures 5¼", and on last row 2, inc 6 sts evenly spaced across row—22 sts.

Establish main patt:

Patt row 1 (RS): K1, RT, (P2, K3, P2, RT) twice, K1.

Rows 2 and 4: K1, P2, (K2, P3, K2, P2) twice, K1.

Row 3: Rep row 1, working all K3 as UC3B.

Rep rows 1–4 until headband is desired length for your head, ending with row 4 and on that last row, dec 6 sts evenly spaced as you BO for

16-st edge to seam to 16-st ribbed edge after blocking.

Block and seam.

VEST INSTRUCTIONS

right and left fronts

With smaller needles and separate balls of yarn, cable CO 53 (57, 65, 69) sts for right and left front at same time.

Row 1 (RS)

Left front: K1 (selvage st), P1, K2, *P2, K2; rep from * to last st, K1 (selvage st).

Right front: K1 (selvage st), *K2, P2; rep from * to last 4 sts, K2, P1, K1 (selvage st).

Row 2

Right front: K1 (selvage st), K1, *P2, K2, rep from * to last 3 sts, P2, K1 (selvage st).

Left front: K1 (selvage st), P2, *K2, P2; rep from * to last 2 sts, K1, K1 (selvage st).

Rep rows 1 and 2 for total of 28 rows; work measures approx 4", ending with WS row.

Next RS row

Left front: K1, M1 kw, *K5, M1 kw; rep from * 4 times, K32 (36, 44, 48).

Right front: K32 (36, 44, 48), *M1 kw, K5; rep from * to last st, M1 kw, K1—58 (62, 70, 74) sts.

Change to larger needles and est main patt as follows:

Row 1 and all WS rows

Right front: K1, K1 (5, 5, 5), P2, K2, P3, K2, P2, K2, P6, K2, (P2, K2) 8 (8, 10, 11) times, P2, K1.

Left front: K1, P2, (K2, P2) 8 (8, 10, 11) times, K2, P6, K2, P2, K2, P3, K2, P2, K1 (5, 5, 5), K1.

Row 2 (RS)

Left front: K1, P1 (5, 5, 5), RT, P2, K3, P2, RT, P2, K6, P2, RT, (P2, K2) 8 (8, 10, 11) times, K1.

Right front: K1, (K2, P2) 8 (8, 10, 11) times, LT, P2, K6, P2, LT, P2, K3, P2, LT, P1 (5, 5, 5), K1.

Row 4

Left front: K1, P1 (5, 5, 5), RT, P2, UC3B, P2, RT, P2, UC6B, P2, RT, (P2, K2) 8 (8, 10, 11) times, K1.

Right front: K1, (K2, P2) 8 (8, 10, 11) times, LT, P2, UC6F, P2, LT, P2, UC3F, P2, LT, P1 (5, 5, 5), K1.

Remember that 3-st uneven cable crosses every 4 rows and 6-st uneven cable crosses every 6 rows.

Cont main patt as est until work measures 14½ (15, 15½, 16)" from beg.

Shape armholes: At side edge, BO 6 (7, 8, 9) sts once. Note that BO will occur on WS row for right front and on RS for left front. **For Small only from this point forward,** work 3-st

cable on RS as K3 on right and left fronts and on WS as K1, P2 for right front and P2, K1 for left front. Cont as est until work measures 16 (16¾, 17½, 18¼)" from beg.

Shape neck: BO 31 (32, 37, 38) sts in patt at neck edge—21 (23, 25, 27) sts. Cont in patt as est until work measures 20¾ (21¾, 22¾, 23¾)" from beg.

Shape shoulders: At shoulder edge, BO 6 (7, 8, 8) sts. Dec 1 st, then BO 6 (7, 7, 8) sts. Dec 1 st, then BO 7 (7, 8, 9) sts.

back

With smaller needles, cable CO 94 (102, 114, 122) sts.

Row 1 (RS): K1 (selvage st), P1, *K2, P2, rep from * to last 4 sts, K2, P1, K1 (selvage st).

Row 2: K1 (selvage st), K1, *P2, K2, rep from * to last 4 sts, P2, K1, K1 (selvage st).

Rep rows 1 and 2 for a total of 28 rows. Work measures approx 4".

Next row: Knit.

Change to larger needles and est main patt as follows.

Row 1 and all WS rows: K1 (selvage st), K1 (5, 5, 5), P2, K2, P3, K2, P2, K2, P6, K2, P2, K2, P3, K2, (P2, K2) 8 (8, 11, 13) times, P3, K2, P2, K2, P6, K2, P2, K2, P3, K2, P2, K1 (5, 5, 5), K1 (selvage st).

Row 2: K1, P1 (5, 5, 5), RT, P2, K3, P2, RT, P2, K6, P2, RT, P2, K3, P2, RT, P2, (K2, P2) 6 (6, 9, 11) times, LT, P2, K3, P2, LT, P2, K6, P2, LT, P2, K3, P2, LT, P1, K1.

Row 4: K1, P1 (5, 5, 5), RT, P2, UC3B, P2, RT, P2, UC6B, P2, RT, P2, UC3B, P2, RT, P2, (K2, P2) 6 (6, 9, 11) times, LT, P2, UC3F, P2, LT, P2, UC6F, P2, LT, P2, UC3F, P2, LT, P1 (5, 5, 5), K1.

Cont as est until work measures 14½ (15, 15½, 16)" from beg.

Shape armholes: BO 6 (7, 8, 9) sts at beg of next 2 rows—82 (88, 98, 104) sts.

Cont in est patt until work measures 20½ (21½, 22½, 23½)" from beg.

Shape neck: Work 29 (31, 35, 37) sts in est patt, BO center 24 (26, 28, 30) sts, and finish row in patt. On next row, beg shoulder shaping as for front and AT SAME TIME attach second ball of yarn to second st at beg of neck edge and cont neck shaping with dec 1 st, then BO 4 (4, 5, 5) sts at beg neck edge of next 2 rows. Dec 1 st, then BO 2 (2, 3, 3) sts at beg neck edge of next 2 rows.

finishing

Meticulously block to measurements.

Seam shoulders using invisible horizontal seaming.

Neck edging: With smaller circular needle, PU 35 (38, 39, 42) sts along 5½ (5¾, 6, 6¼)" vertical left neck edge, PU 40 (42, 48, 50) sts at back of neck, PU 35 (38, 39, 42) sts along 5½ (5¾, 6, 6¼)" vertical right neck edge—110 (118, 126, 134) sts.

Row 1 (RS): *K2, P2; rep from * to last 2 sts, K2.

Row 2: *P2, K2; rep from * to last 2 sts, P2.

Work a total of 42 rows and BO in patt on next row.

Steam block collar one half at a time.

Seam front collar horizontal edges using invisible vertical to horizontal seaming. On right front of collar, leave an opening 1" inside outer edge in size appropriate to accommodate button you have selected.

Seam sides using invisible vertical seaming.

Sleeve edging: Using smaller circular needle, PU 92 (100, 108, 116) sts.

Rnds 1–10: *K2, P2; rep from * to end.

Rnd 11: BO in patt.

Sew button in place on left side, 1" from outer edge.

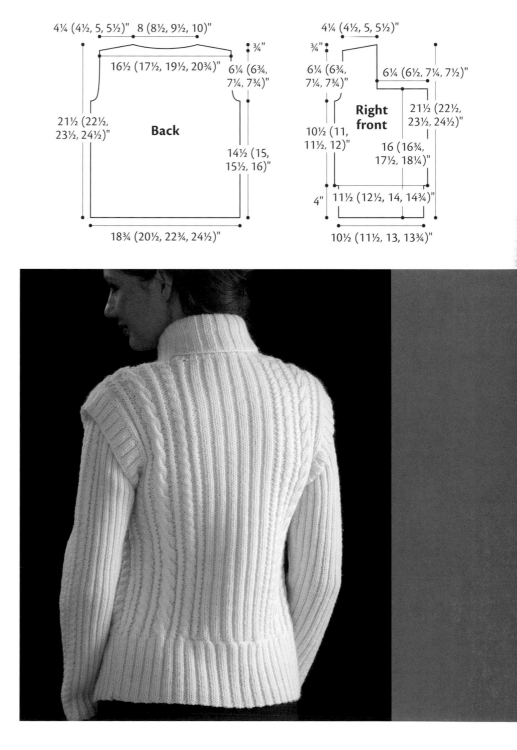

Back

4¼ (4½, 5, 5½)" 8 (8½, 9½, 10)"

¾"

16½ (17½, 19½, 20¾)"

6¼ (6¾, 7¼, 7¾)"

21½ (22½, 23½, 24½)"

14½ (15, 15½, 16)"

18¾ (20½, 22¾, 24½)"

Right front

4¼ (4½, 5, 5½)"

¾"

6¼ (6¾, 7¼, 7¾)" 6¼ (6½, 7¼, 7½)"

10½ (11, 11½, 12)"

21½ (22½, 23½, 24½)"

16 (16¾, 17½, 18¼)"

4" 11½ (12½, 14, 14¾)"

10½ (11½, 13, 13¾)"

twisted rib and cable DRESS or PULLOVER and WRISTLETS

Indulge in this long and lean dress, or if you prefer, make it as a fabulous pullover sweater. With its interesting twisted ribbing and cable for texture and its cozy overlapped banded collar, it's certain to be a favorite. Wristlets can accent the sleeves or be worn with whatever suits your fancy.

Skill Level: Intermediate ■■■◻

Size: Small (Medium, Large, Extra Large)

Finished Measurements

Bust: 40 (44, 48, 52)"

Dress Length: 35½ (36, 36½, 37)"

Pullover Length: 21¾ (23¼, 24¾, 26¼)"

MATERIALS

Nature Spun Sportweight from Brown Sheep Company (100% wool; 1.75 oz/50 g; 184 yds/168 m) 🔲2

Dress: 9 (10, 11, 12) skeins in color 110 Blueberry

Pullover: 7 (8, 9, 10) skeins in color N30S Nordic Blue

Wristlets: approx ½ skein in color to match dress or pullover

Size 4 (3.5 mm) and 5 (3.75 mm) needles or size required to obtain gauge

Cable needle

GAUGE

24 sts and 32 rows = 4" in combination of patt on larger needles

PATTERN STITCHES

Twisted Rib Cable

See chart on page 59.

(Multiple of 7 sts)

Row 1 and all WS rows: (P1 tbl, K1) 3 times, P1 tbl.

Rows 2, 4, 8, and 10: (K1 tbl, P1) 3 times, K1 tbl.

Row 6: Sl 4 sts to cn and hold in back, K1 tbl, P1, K1 tbl, (P1, K1 tbl) twice from cn.

Rep rows 1–6 for sweater and rows 1–10 for dress.

Twisted Linked Cable

See chart on page 59.

(Multiple of 5 sts)

T2FP (twist 2 front purl): Sl 1 st to cn and hold in front, P1, K1 tbl from cn.

T2BP (twist 2 back purl): Sl 1 st to cn and hold in back, K1 tbl, P1 from cn.

T3BP (twist 3 back purl): Sl 2 sts to cn and hold in back, K1 tbl, (P1, K1 tbl) from cn.

Rows 1 and 3: (WS): P1 tbl, (K1, P1 tbl) twice.

Row 2: K1 tbl, (P1, K1 tbl) twice.

Row 4: T2FP, K1 tbl, T2BP.

Rows 5 and 7: K1, P1 tbl 3 times, K1.

Row 6: P1, T3BP, P1.

Row 8: T2BP, K1 tbl, T2FP.

Rep rows 1–8 for patt.

Medium: K2, 5 sts in twisted linked cable (row 1), *K2, P1 tbl, K2, 7 sts in twisted rib cable (row 1), K2, P1 tbl, K2, 5 sts in twisted linked cable (row 1)*, rep from * to * once, K2, P1 tbl, K2, 7 sts in twisted rib cable, K2, P1 tbl, K1, P1 tbl, K2, 7 sts in twisted rib cable, K2, P1 tbl, K2, 5 sts in twisted linked cable, rep from * to * once more, K2, P1 tbl, K2, 7 sts in twisted rib cable, K2, P1 tbl, K2, 5 sts in twisted linked cable (row 1), K2.

Large: K2, (P1 tbl, K2) twice, 5 sts in twisted linked cable (row 1), *K2, P1 tbl, K2, 7 sts in twisted rib cable (row 1), K2, P1 tbl, K2, 5 sts in twisted linked cable (row 1)*, rep from * to * once, K2, P1 tbl, K2, 7 sts in twisted rib cable, K2, P1 tbl, K1, P1 tbl, K2, 7 sts in twisted rib cable, K2, P1 tbl, K2, 5 sts in twisted linked cable, rep from * to * once more, K2, P1 tbl, K2, 7 sts in twisted rib cable, K2, P1 tbl, K2, 5 sts in twisted linked cable, (K2, P1 tbl) twice, K2.

Extra Large: K2, 7 sts in twisted rib cable (row 1), K2, P1 tbl, K2, 5 sts in twisted linked cable (row 1), *K2, P1 tbl, K2, 7 sts in twisted rib cable (row 1), K2, P1 tbl, K2, 5 sts in twisted linked cable (row 1)*, rep from * to * once, K2, P1 tbl, K2, 7 sts in twisted rib cable, K2, P1 tbl, K1, P1 tbl, K2, 7 sts in twisted rib cable, K2, P1 tbl, K2, 5 sts in twisted linked cable, rep from * to * once more, K2, P1 tbl, K2, 7 sts in twisted rib cable, K2, P1 tbl, K2, 5 sts in twisted linked cable, K2, P1 tbl, K2, 7 sts in twisted rib cable, K2.

Row 2 (RS)

Small: K1, *P2, K1 tbl, P2, 7 sts in twisted rib cable (row 2), P2, K1 tbl, P2, 5 sts in twisted linked cable (row

DRESS OR PULLOVER INSTRUCTIONS

back

With smaller needles, cable CO 121 (133, 145, 157) sts and work bottom ribbing as follows.

Row 1 (RS): K1 (selvage st), *P3, K1 tbl; rep from * to last 4 sts, P3, K1 (selvage st).

Row 2: K1 (selvage st), *K3, P1 tbl; rep from * to last 4 sts, K3, K1 (selvage st).

Rep rows 1 and 2 through row 11.

Change to larger needles and est main patt as follows.

Row 1 (WS)

Small: K1, *K2, P1 tbl, K2, 7 sts in twisted rib cable (row 1), K2, P1 tbl, K2, 5 sts in twisted linked cable (row 1)*, rep from * to * once, K2, P1 tbl, K2, 7 sts in twisted rib cable, K2, P1 tbl, K1, P1 tbl, K2, 7 sts in twisted rib cable, K2, P1 tbl, K2, 5 sts in twisted linked cable, rep from * to * once more, K2, P1 tbl, K2, 7 sts in twisted rib cable, K2, P1 tbl, K2, K1.

2)*, rep from * to * once, P2, K1 tbl, P2, 7 sts in twisted rib cable, P2, K1 tbl, P1, K1 tbl, P2, 7 sts in twisted rib cable, P2, K1 tbl, P2, 5 sts in twisted linked cable, rep from * to * once more, P2, K1 tbl, P2, 7 sts in twisted rib cable, P2, K1 tbl, P2, K1.

Medium: K1, P1, 5 sts in twisted linked cable (row 2), *P2, K1 tbl, P2, 7 sts in twisted rib cable (row 2), P2, K1 tbl, P2, 5 sts in twisted linked cable (row 2)*, rep from * to * once, P2, K1 tbl, P2, 7 sts in twisted rib cable, P2, K1 tbl, P1, K1 tbl, P2, 7 sts in twisted rib cable, P2, K1 tbl, P2, 5 sts in twisted linked cable, rep from * to * once more, P2, K1 tbl, P2, 7 sts in twisted rib cable, P2, K1 tbl, P2, 5 sts in twisted linked cable, P1, K1.

Large: K1, P1, K1 tbl, P2, K1 tbl, P2, 5 sts in twisted linked cable (row 2), *P2, K1 tbl, P2, 7 sts in twisted rib cable (row 2), P2, K1 tbl, P2, 5 sts in twisted linked cable (row 2)*, rep from * to * once, P2, K1 tbl, P2, 7 sts in twisted rib cable, P2, K1 tbl, P1, K1 tbl, P2, 7 sts in twisted rib cable, P2, K1 tbl, P2, 5 sts in twisted linked cable, rep from * to * once more, P2, K1 tbl, P2, 7 sts in twisted rib cable, P2, K1 tbl, P2, 5 sts in twisted linked cable, P2, K1 tbl, P2, K1 tbl, P1, K1.

Extra Large: K1, P1, 7 sts in twisted rib cable (row 2), P2, K1 tbl, P2, 5 sts in twisted linked cable (row 2), *P2, K1 tbl, P2, 7 sts in twisted rib cable (row 2), P2, K1 tbl, P2, 5 sts in twisted linked cable (row 2)*, rep from * to * once, P2, K1 tbl, P2, 7 sts in twisted rib cable, P2, K1 tbl, P1, K1 tbl, P2, 7 sts in twisted rib cable, P2, K1 tbl, P2, 5 sts in twisted linked cable, rep from * to * once more, P2, K1 tbl, P2, 7 sts in twisted rib cable, P2, K1 tbl, P2, 5 sts in twisted linked cable, P2, K1 tbl, P2, 7 sts in twisted rib cable, P1, K1.

Pullover: Work even in est patt for a total of 98 (106, 114, 122) rows in main patt and until work measures approx 13½ (14½, 15½, 16½)" from beg—109 (117, 125, 133) rows total including ribbing.

Dress: Work even in est patt for a total of 208 rows in main patt and work measures approx 27¼" from beg—219 rows total including ribbing.

> **CHANGING LENGTH**
>
> If you wish to change the length, do so before shaping armholes.

Shape armholes: BO 4 (5, 6, 6) sts at beg of next 2 rows. Dec 1 st, then BO 2 (2, 2, 3) sts at beg of next 2 rows—107 (117, 127, 137) sts. Note that after armhole shaping, work first 6 sts of WS rows as K2, (P1 tbl, K1) twice, and work last 6 sts as (K1, P1 tbl) twice, K2; on RS rows, work first 6 sts as K1, P1, (K1 tbl, P1) twice, and work last 6 sts as (P1, K1 tbl) twice, P1, K1. Work even to armhole depth of 7½ (8, 8½, 9)".

Shape shoulders: BO 9 (10, 11, 11) sts at beg of next 2 rows. Dec 1 st, then BO 8 (9, 10, 11) sts at beg of next 2 rows. Dec 1 st, then BO 9 (10, 11, 12) sts at beg of next 2 rows. BO rem 51 (55, 59, 65) sts.

front

Work as for back, and beg neck shaping on same row that armhole shaping beg, BO 1 center st and attach a second ball of yarn.

Next row (RS):

Left side of V-neck: Work to last 4 sts, P2tog, sl next st to cn and hold in back, K1 tbl from left needle, P1 from cn.

Right side of V-neck: With second ball of yarn, work first 4 sts as sl 1 to cn and hold in front, P1 from left needle, K1 tbl from cn, P2tog, work in patt to end of row.

Next row (WS): Work 1 row even across right and left front.

V-neck decs:

Left side: Work to last 4 sts, then P2tog, K1 tbl, K1 (selvage st).

Right side: Work first 4 sts as K1 (selvage st), K1 tbl, P2tog, work in patt to end of row.

Rep V-neck decs EOR another 19 (21, 23, 26) times, then work same dec every 4 rows 4 times more. End with shoulder shaping as for back.

sleeves

With smaller needles, cable CO 59 (63, 67, 71) sts.

Row 1 (RS): K1 (selvage st), P2, *K1 tbl, P3, rep from * to last 4 sts, K1 tbl, P2, K1 (selvage st).

Row 2: K1 (selvage st), K2, *P1 tbl, K3, rep from * to last 4 sts, P1 tbl, K2, K1 (selvage st).

Rep rows 1 and 2 through row 11.

Change to larger needles and est main patt as follows.

Row 1 (WS): K1, K0 (0, 0, 2), P1 tbl, (K1, P1 tbl) 1 (2, 3, 3) time, K2, P1 tbl, K2, 5 sts in twisted linked cable (row 1), K2, P1 tbl, K2, 7 sts in twisted rib cable (row 1), K2, P1 tbl, K1, P1 tbl, K2, 7 sts in twisted rib cable, K2, P1 tbl, K2, 5 sts in twisted linked cable, K2, P1 tbl, K2, (P1 tbl, K1) 1 (2, 3, 3) time, P1 tbl (note that this is st 7 of twisted rib cable row 1 for Extra Large), K0 (0, 0, 2), K1—59 (63, 67, 71) sts.

Row 2: K1, P0 (0, 0, 2), K1 tbl, (P1, K1 tbl) 1 (2, 3, 3) time, P2, K1 tbl, P2, 5 sts in twisted linked cable (row 2), P2, K1 tbl, P2, 7 sts in twisted rib cable (row 2), P2, K1 tbl, P1, K1 tbl, P2, 7 sts in twisted rib cable, P2, K1 tbl, P2, 5 sts in twisted linked cable, P2, K1 tbl, P2, (K1 tbl, P1) 1 (2, 3, 3) time, K1 tbl, P0 (0, 0, 2), K1.

Work even in est patt.

Shape sleeves: Beg with row 10 (10, 12, 4), inc 1 st at each edge using M1 pw inside selvage sts. Rep this inc every 10 rows 5 (5, 0, 0) times more, and every 8 rows a total of 7 (8, 14, 15) times—85 (91, 97, 103) sts.

For Small (Medium), when 4 (2) incs have been worked, establish 7-st cable on 7 sts at outer edges of sleeve inside selvage sts. For Large and Extra Large, 7 sts inside selvage sts are already set up for 7-st cable. Once 7-st cables are est at outer edges, work all rem incs as (K1 tbl, P2) on RS and (P1 tbl, K2) on WS rows and cont to add incs in this patt only from that point on.

Work even through main patt row 124 (126, 130, 130).

Shape caps: BO 4 (5, 6, 6) sts at beg of next 2 rows. Dec 1 st, then BO 2 (2, 2, 3) sts at beg of next 2 rows. Dec 1 st at each edge EOR 4 (6, 8, 10) times. Dec 1 st at each edge of next 18 rows. Dec 1 st, then BO 1 st at beg of next 2 rows. Dec 1 st, then BO 2 sts at beg of next 2 rows. BO rem 17 sts.

collar

With smaller needles, cable CO 23 sts.

Row 1 (RS): K1 (selvage st), P1, *K1 tbl, P2, rep from * to last 3 sts, K1 tbl, P1, K1 (selvage st).

Row 2: K1 (selvage st), K1, *P1 tbl, K2, rep from * to last 3 sts, P1 tbl, K1, K1 (selvage st).

Rep rows 1 and 2. Work to 23 (24¾, 26¼, 28¼)" and BO.

finishing

Meticulously block to measurements.

Sew shoulder seams, matching patt sts and using invisible horizontal seaming, referring to "Joining Textured Shoulders" on page 12.

Set in sleeves using invisible vertical to horizontal seaming.

Sew side and underarm seams using invisible vertical seaming.

Sew collar: Sew 1 short edge of collar band to 1 edge of V at base of neck using invisible vertical to horizontal seaming. Sew other short edge to beginning of long edge already anchored by short edge using same seaming to close collar band. Sew rem long edge to rem V-neck, pinning evenly to shoulder seaming. Pin rem length to back of neck easing in any fullness and seam.

Twisted rib cable

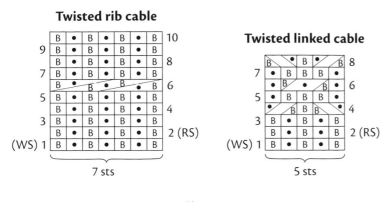

7 sts

Twisted linked cable

5 sts

Key

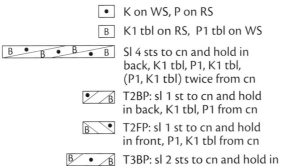

- ⋅ K on WS, P on RS
- B K1 tbl on RS, P1 tbl on WS
- Sl 4 sts to cn and hold in back, K1 tbl, P1, K1 tbl, (P1, K1 tbl) twice from cn
- T2BP: sl 1 st to cn and hold in back, K1 tbl, P1 from cn
- T2FP: sl 1 st to cn and hold in front, P1, K1 tbl from cn
- T3BP: sl 2 sts to cn and hold in back, K1 tbl, (P1, K1 tbl) from cn

WRISTLETS INSTRUCTIONS

wristlets

With smaller needles, CO 25 sts using the backward loop CO. (See page 75.)

Row 1 (RS): K1 (selvage st), *P2, K1 tbl, rep from * to last 3 sts, P2, K1 (selvage st).

Row 2: K1 (selvage st), *K2, P1 tbl, rep from * to last 3 sts, K2, K1 (selvage st).

Rep to desired length for your wrist, approx 7 (7½, 8, 8½)".

finishing

Transfer live sts to waste yarn or circular needle to steam block, then transfer back.

Sl second needle through loops of CO row, picking up 1 loop for each CO st.

Fold piece with RS tog and use 3-needle BO to join seam.

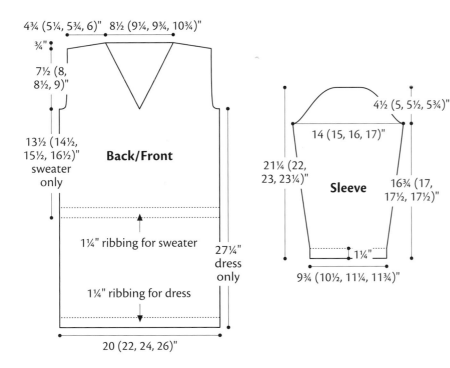

arrowhead lace
CARDIGAN and SHELL

Skill Level

Cardigan: Experienced ◼◼◼◼

Shell: Intermediate ◼◼◼◻

Size: Small (Medium, Large, Extra Large)

Finished Measurements

Cardigan Bust: 37½ (42½, 47½, 52½)"

Cardigan Length: 22½ (23, 24¾, 25¼)"

Shell Bust: 34 (37½, 40½, 44)"

Shell Length: 20¼ (21¼, 22¼, 23¼)"

MATERIALS

Butterfly Super 10 from Kertzer (100% mercerized cotton; 125 g; 230 m) in color 3818 ⓼

  Cardigan: 4 (5, 5, 6) skeins

  Shell: 2 (3, 3, 3) skeins

Size 6 (4 mm) needles or size required to obtain gauge

Size 6 (4 mm) circular needles (32" for cardigan neck edging, 18" for shell sleeve edging)

GAUGE

16 sts and 28 rows = 4" in arrowhead lace patt when blocked

18 sts and 28 rows = 4" in St st when blocked

PATTERN STITCH

Arrowhead Lace Pattern

See chart A on page 64.

(Multiple of 10 sts + 1 st)

Row 1 (RS): K1, *(YO, sl 1 kw-K1-psso) twice, K1, (K2tog, YO) twice, K1; rep from * across.

Row 2: K1, purl to last st, K1.

Row 3: K1, *K1, YO, sl 1 kw-K1-psso, YO, sl 1 kw-K2tog-psso, YO, K2tog, YO, K2; rep from * across.

Row 4: K1, purl to last st, K1.

Rep rows 1–4 for patt.

Right Half Lace Repeat

See chart B on page 64.

(Worked over 5 sts.)

Row 1 (RS): K1, (K2tog, YO) twice.

Row 2: P5.

Row 3: K2, K2tog, YO, K1.

Row 4: P5.

Rep rows 1–4 for patt.

Left Half Lace Repeat

See chart C on page 64.

(Worked over 5 sts.)

Row 1 (RS): (YO, sl 1 kw-K1-psso) twice, K1.

Row 2: P5.

Row 3: K1, (YO, sl 1 kw-K1-psso) twice.

Row 4: P5.

Rep rows 1–4 for patt.

This light and airy cotton cardigan is finished with picot edges. The sleeves flare ever so slightly. The fitted shell is worked in stockinette stitch, with the yoke worked in the arrowhead lace pattern.

CARDIGAN INSTRUCTIONS

back

Cable CO 75 (85, 95, 105) sts.

Work hem as follows.

Rows 1–5: Work 5 rows in St st with garter st selvage, beg with purl row.

Row 6 (RS): K1, *YO, K2tog, rep from * to end. This is fold line for hem.

Rows 7–10: Work 4 rows in St st with garter st selvage, beg with purl row.

Row 11: Knit.

Row 12: K1, purl to last st, K1.

Note that the hem was knit wrong side out and later will be folded to the RS with hemmed edge facing the RS. From this point forward, odd-numbered rows are on the right side.

Beg arrowhead lace patt:

Row 1 (RS): K2, work row 1 of arrowhead lace patt (chart A) to last 2 sts, K2.

Row 2: K1, purl to last st (row 2 of chart A), K1.

Keeping first 2 and last 2 sts as est, cont chart A until piece measures 14¼ (14¼, 15½, 15½)" from beg of lace patt. End after completing row 4 of arrowhead lace patt.

SHAPING NOTE

As you work the armhole shaping, keep the first and last 2 or 3 sts in St st. Work a YO only if there is a corresponding decrease, and vice versa. BO kw on RS rows and pw on WS rows. See "Decreases" on page 75 for tips on creating smooth edges.

Shape armholes: BO 3 (5, 7, 9) sts at beg of row, K3, work in patt to end of row. On next row, BO 3 (5, 7, 9) sts at beg of row, purl across. Dec 1 st, then BO 1 (1, 3, 3) st at beg of next 2 rows—65 (71, 73, 79) sts.

Work even in patt as est until armhole measures 7¼ (7¾, 8¼, 8¾)".

Shape shoulders: Note that you should not work a YO or dec in the last RS row for sts that form the step of the shoulder shaping on the next WS row. Instead, work the number of sts that form the WS shoulder shaping in St st on previous RS row. BO 6 (7, 7, 8) sts at beg of next 2 rows. Dec 1 st, then BO 6 (7, 7, 8) sts at beg of next 4 rows. Place rem 25 (25, 27, 27) sts on holder for back neck.

right front

Work the right and left fronts at the same time with separate balls of yarn to ensure that you have the same number of pattern repeats on both pieces.

Cable CO 35 (40, 45, 50) sts.

Work hem rows 1–12 as for back.

Beg arrowhead lace patt:

Row 1 (RS): K2, work first 0 (5, 0, 5) sts following row 1 of right edge half rep (chart B), work row 1 of chart A to last 2 sts, K2.

Row 2: K1, purl to last st (row 2 of charts A and B), K1.

Keeping first 2 and last 2 sts as est, work charts A and B until piece measures 10¾ (10¾, 11½, 11½)".

SHAPING NOTE

Neck and armholes are shaped at the same time. Read all instructions before continuing with knitting. See "Necklines" on page 13.

Shape neck and armholes: Dec 1 st using ssk inside neck edge between st at inner edge and beg of patt st on next RS row, then every following 8 rows 9 (9, 10, 10) times. AT SAME TIME when piece measures same as back to armhole, shape armholes as for back.

Work even in patt as est until armhole measures same as back to shoulder—20 (23, 23, 26) sts rem after neck and armhole shaping are complete.

Shape shoulder as for back.

left front

Cable CO 35 (40, 45, 50) sts.

Work hem rows 1–12 as for back.

Beg arrowhead lace patt:

Row 1 (RS): K2, work row 1 of chart A to last 2 (7, 2, 7) sts, work next 0 (5, 0, 5) sts following row 1 of left edge half rep (chart C), K2.

Row 2: K1, purl to last st (row 2 of charts A and C), K1.

Keeping first 2 and last 2 sts as est, cont charts A and C until piece measures 10¾ (10¾, 11½, 11½)".

Shape neck and armholes: Dec 1 st using K2tog inside neck edge between patt st and st at inner edge on next RS row, then every following 8 rows 9 (9, 10, 10) times. AT SAME TIME when piece measures same as back to armhole, shape armholes as for back.

Work even in patt as est until armhole measures same as back to shoulder—20 (23, 23, 26) sts rem after neck and armhole shaping are complete.

Shape shoulder as for back.

sleeves

Work both sleeves at the same time with separate balls of yarn to ensure that you have the same number of pattern repeats on both pieces.

Cable CO 39 (39, 49, 49) sts.

Work rows 1–12 as for back.

Beg arrowhead lace patt:

Row 1 (RS): K4, work row 1 of arrowhead lace patt (chart A) to last 4 sts, K4.

Rows 2 and 4: K1, purl to last st (row 2 of chart A), K1.

Keeping first 4 and last 4 sts as est, cont chart A for 6 (6, 10, 10) more rows.

Shape sleeves: Dec 1 st at each edge every 8 rows a total of 3 times by working dec rows with ssk at beg of row, work in patt as est to last 2 sts, K2tog at end of row—33 (33, 43, 43) sts.

Inc 1 st at each edge using M1 kw inside selvage sts every 8 rows a total of 4 (6, 3, 5) times and every 12 rows a total of 4 times—49 (53, 57, 61) sts.

WORKING INCREASES INTO PATTERN

*Work sleeve inc in St st until you have 5 sts inside selvage, then work right edge half rep (chart B) at beg of row and left edge half rep (chart C) at end of row. Work additional sleeve inc in St st until you have 5 more sts inside selvage, then work arrowhead lace patt across between selvages. Rep from * until all incs have been worked.

Work even in patt as est until sleeve measures approx 16 (16, 17, 17)" from beg of arrowhead lace patt, or desired length to underarm. End after row 4 of arrowhead lace patt.

Sleeve caps: BO 3 (3, 4, 4) sts at beg of next 2 rows. Dec 1 st, then BO 1 (1, 1, 2) st at beg of next 2 rows. Dec 1 st at each edge on next row and every fourth row another 4 (5, 6, 7) times, using ssk at beg of row and K2tog at end of row. Work 3 rows even. Dec 1 st, then BO 1 st at beg of next 4 rows. Dec 1, then BO 2 sts at beg of next 2 rows. BO rem 15 (17, 17, 17) sts.

finishing

Meticulously block pieces to measurements, opening up lace sts.

Sew shoulder seams using invisible horizontal seaming.

Sew sleeves into armholes using invisible vertical to horizontal seaming.

Sew side seams and underarm seams using invisible vertical seaming. Turn edging toward main patt and seam from RS, sewing in and out of CO loops.

Front edges and back neck: Using 32"-long, size 6 circular needle, with WS of work facing you and beg at right-lower edge, PU 102 (102, 112, 112) sts, place 25 (25, 27, 27) back neck sts from holder on circular needle, PU 102 (102, 112, 112) sts on left front edge—229 (229, 251, 251) sts total. Work bands as follows.

Rows 1 and 3 (RS): Knit.

Rows 2 and 4: K1, purl to last st, K1.

Row 5: K1, *YO, K2tog; rep from * to last st, K1. This is fold line for neck.

Rows 6, 8, and 10: Rep row 2.

Rows 7 and 9: Rep row 1.

Row 11: BO all sts kw.

Steam block this edging on an ironing board in sections (or one half at a time). Fold and pin hems in place from front and back of neck edge as well as from cuffs. Sew in and out of CO loops for cuffs, and BO loops for fronts and back of neck edges to seam. Note that if you BO too tightly or seam too tightly through loops, the edges will pucker.

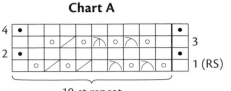

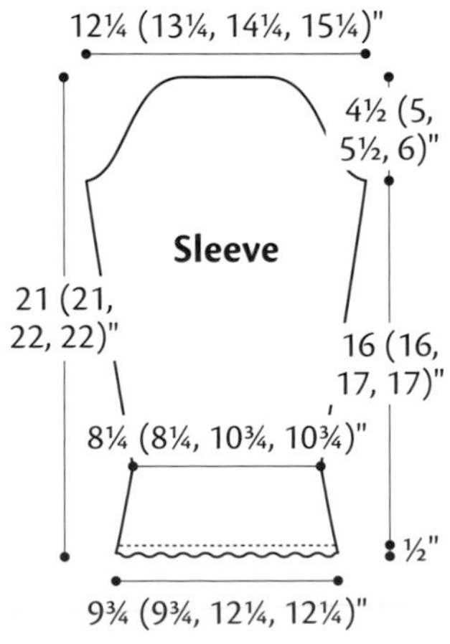

Chart A

10-st repeat

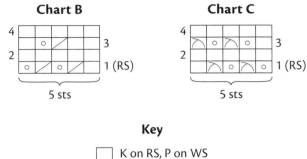

Chart B

5 sts

Chart C

5 sts

Key

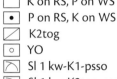

☐ K on RS, P on WS
• P on RS, K on WS
◩ K2tog
○ YO
⌒ Sl 1 kw-K1-psso
⌒ Sl 1 kw-K2tog-psso

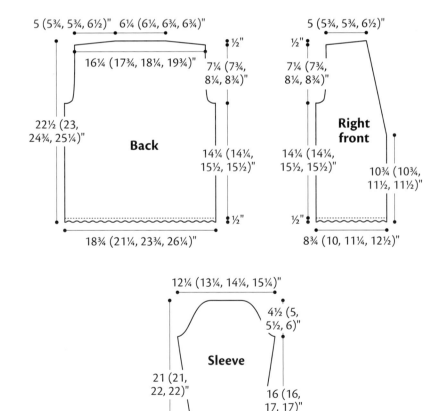

5 (5¾, 5¾, 6½)"   6¼ (6¼, 6¾, 6¾)"   5 (5¾, 5¾, 6½)"

½"   ½"

16¼ (17¾, 18¼, 19¾)"   7¼ (7¾, 8¼, 8¾)"   7¼ (7¾, 8¼, 8¾)"

22½ (23, 24¾, 25¼)"   **Back**   **Right front**

14¼ (14¼, 15½, 15½)"   14¼ (14¼, 15½, 15½)"   10¾ (10¾, 11½, 11½)"

½"   ½"

18¾ (21¼, 23¾, 26¼)"   8¾ (10, 11¼, 12½)"

12¼ (13¼, 14¼, 15¼)"

4½ (5, 5½, 6)"

Sleeve

21 (21, 22, 22)"   16 (16, 17, 17)"

8¼ (8¼, 10¾, 10¾)"

½"

9¾ (9¾, 12¼, 12¼)"

SHELL INSTRUCTIONS

front and back

Cable CO 77 (85, 91, 99) sts and work rows 1–12 as for cardigan back. Cont in St st (rep rows 11 and 12) until work measures 4½ (4¾, 5¼, 5½)" from fold line of hem; approx 38 (40, 42, 44) rows.

Shape waist: On next row, dec 1 st at each edge inside selvage sts, then rep this dec 3 more times every 6 rows. Beg row 63 (65, 67, 69), inc 1 st using M1 kw at each edge inside selvage sts, then rep this inc 3 more times every 6 rows. Work even to 13 (13½, 14, 14½)", or approx 96 (100, 104, 108) rows total.

Shape armholes: BO 4 (4, 5, 5) sts at beg of next 2 rows. Dec 1 st, then BO 1 (1, 2, 2) st at beg of next 2 rows—65 (73, 75, 83) sts.

Change to arrowhead lace patt st and work first row 1 only as follows to achieve decs:

Row 101 (105, 109, 113): K3 (2, 3, 2), ([YO, sl 1 kw-K1-psso] twice, K1, [K2tog, YO] twice, K1) 0 (1, 1, 1) times, *(YO, sl 1 kw-K2tog-psso) twice, K1, (K2tog, YO) twice, K1; rep from * 4 more times, ([YO, sl 1 kw-K1-psso] twice, K1, [K2tog, YO] twice, K1) 0 (0, 0, 1) times, end K2 (1, 2, 1)—55 (63, 65, 73) sts.

Cont for another 43 (47, 49, 53) rows as follows: K2 (1, 2, 1), work chart A to last 2 (1, 2, 1) sts, end K2 (1, 2, 1).

Rows 145–147 (153–155, 159–161, 167–169): Work 2 rows in St st and BO on next row; armhole should measure approx 7¼ (7¾, 8¼, 8¾)".

finishing

Meticulously block pieces to measurements, opening up lace sts. Steam block with bottom edging folded and pinned into place.

Sew side seams and underarm seams using invisible vertical seaming. Turn edging toward main patt and seam from RS, sewing in and out of CO loops.

Sew shoulder seams to width of 1½" using invisible horizontal seaming.

Sew hem in place as given for cardigan.

Armhole edging: With 18"-long, size 6 circular needle, PU 70 (74, 78, 82) sts and knit 2 rnds. BO all sts on next rnd.

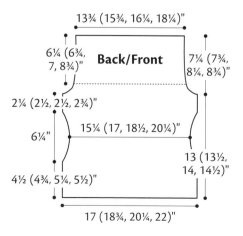

chain and double cable
CARDIGAN and SOCKS

For those who have a penchant for cables, these fun cables and details say it all in the happiest of colors. The knotted cable used for the collar, cuff, and bottom ribbing is a manipulation of other knotted cables I have seen. This interpretation adds a tassel-like effect at the outer edge of the knot. It is the first cable pattern I have come across that utilizes two cable needles. It could also be worked with one cable needle by slipping stitches from the cable needle back to the left-hand needle. I found it somewhat simpler and quicker to use two cable needles. It is fun to work and no more difficult than working with one cable needle.

Skill Level: Experienced ■■■■

Sizes

Cardigan: Small (Medium, Large, Extra Large)

Socks: Small/Medium (Large/Extra Large)

Finished Measurements

Cardigan Bust: 38 (43, 48, 51)"

Cardigan Length: 23 (24, 25, 26)"

Sock Length: Approx 6½" will fit womens' shoe size 6 (7), work additional length as needed

MATERIALS

Nature Spun Sportweight from Brown Sheep Company (100% wool; 1.75 oz/50g; 184 yds/168 m) in color 105 Bougainvillea ■2■

　Cardigan: 9 (10, 11, 12) skeins

　Socks: 2 (2) skeins

Size 4 (3.5 mm) and 5 (3.75 mm) needles or size required to obtain gauge

Size 3 (3.25 mm) and 4 (3.5 mm) circular needles (32"), plus one extra size 3 needle for 3-needle BO

2 cable needles

12 (14, 14, 15) buttons, ⅝" diameter

18 (20, 22, 24)" of ⅝"-wide gros-grain ribbon in matching color. (See "Ribbon" on page 14.)

Thread in matching color for sewing ribbon and buttons

GAUGE

27 sts and 36 rows = 4" in main patt sts on size 5 needles when blocked

PATTERN STITCHES

Double Cable (also known as Horseshoe Cable)

See chart on page 72.

(Multiple of 12 sts)

C4B (cable 4 back): Sl 2 sts to cn and hold at back of work, K2, K2 from cn.

C4F (cable 4 front): Sl 2 sts to cn and hold at front, K2, K2 from cn.

Rows 1, 3, 5, and 7 (WS): K2, P8, K2.

Rows 2 and 6: P2, K8, P2.

Row 4: P2, C4B, C4F, P2.

Row 8: P2, K8, P2.

Chain and Double Cable

See chart on page 72.

(Multiple of 12 sts)

C4B and C4F: See above.

T4B (twist 4 back): Sl 2 sts to cn and hold at back, K2, P2 from cn.

T4F (twist 4 front): Sl 2 sts to cn and hold at front, P2, K2 from cn.

T3B (twist 3 back): Sl 1 st to cn and hold at back, K2, P1 from cn.

T3F (twist 3 front): Sl 2 sts to cn and hold at front, P1, K2 from cn.

Rows 1, 3, 5, and 7 (WS): K2, P8, K2.

Rows 2 and 6: P2, K8, P2.

Row 4: P2, C4B, C4F, P2.

Row 8: P2, T4B, T4F, P2.

Rows 9 and 15: K2, P2, K4, P2, K2.

Row 10: P1, T3B, P4, T3F, P1.

Rows 11 and 13: K1, P2, K6, P2, K1.

Row 12: P1, K2, P6, K2, P1.

Row 14: P1, T3F, P4, T3B, P1.

Row 16: P2, C4F, C4B, P2.

CHAIN AND DOUBLE CABLE CARDIGAN AND SOCKS

Right Twist (RT)

K2tog, leaving sts on left-hand needle, insert right-hand needle from the front between the 2 sts just knit tog and knit the first st again, then sl both sts from left-hand to right-hand needle.

Left Twist (LT)

With right-hand needle behind left-hand needle, sk 1 st and knit the second st tbl, then insert right-hand needle into the back of both sts (skipped st and second st) and K2tog tbl.

SELVAGE STITCHES

Selvage stitches are identified in parentheses in the first two rows of the pattern and are included in the instructions for the following rows without being labeled as such.

CARDIGAN INSTRUCTIONS

back

With size 4 needles, cable CO 127 (145, 163, 172) sts. Work ribbing as follows.

Row 1 (RS): K1 (selvage st), P1, *K2, P2, K2, P3; rep from * to last 8 sts, K2, P2, K2, P1, K1 (selvage st).

Row 2: K1 (selvage st), K1, *P2, K2, P2, K3; rep from * to last 8 sts, P2, K2, P2, K1, K1 (selvage st).

Rows 3–8: Rep rows 1 and 2.

Row 9: K1, P1, *sl 2 sts to cn and hold at back, sl 2 sts to cn and hold at front, P2tog, K2 from cn at front, P2tog from cn at back, P3; rep from *, end last rep with P1, K1 instead of P3—99 (113, 127, 134) sts.

Row 10: K3, *P2, K5, rep from * to last 5 sts, P2, K3.

Row 11: K1, P2, *K2, P5, rep from * to last 5 sts, K2, P2, K1.

Row 12: K2, *sl 1 st to cn and hold at front, sl 2 sts to cn hold at back, P1f&b, K2 from cn at back, P1f&b from cn at front, K3, rep from *, end last rep with K2 instead of K3—127 (145, 163, 172) sts.

Rows 13–22: Rep rows 1 and 2.

Rows 23–26: Rep rows 9–12.

Row 27: Knit.

Change to larger needles and est main patts as follows.

Row 1 (WS)

Small: K1, K4, *P2, 12 sts in double cable (row 1), P2, 12 sts in chain and double cable (row 1)*, rep from * to *, P2, K1, P2, 12 sts in chain and double cable, rep from * to *, P2, 12 sts in double cable, P2, K4, K1.

Medium: K1, K5, P2, *K1, 12 sts in double cable (row 1), K1, P2, K1, 12 sts in chain and double cable (row 1)*, K1, P2, rep from * to *, K1, P2, K1, P2, K1, 12 sts in chain and double cable, K1, P2, rep from * to *, K1, P2, K1, 12 sts in double cable, K1, P2, K5, K1.

Large: K1, K8, *P2, 12 sts in chain and double cable (row 1), P2, 12 sts in double cable (row 1)*, rep from * to *, P2, 12 sts in chain and double cable, P2, K1, rep from * to * twice, P2, 12 sts in chain and double cable, P2, K8, K1.

Extra Large: K2, *K1, P2, K1, 12 sts in chain and double cable (row 1), K1, P2, K1, 12 sts in double cable (row 1)*, rep from * to *, K1, P2, K1, 12 sts in chain and double cable, K1, P2, K1, rep from * to * twice, K1, P2, K1, 12 sts in chain and double cable, K1, P2, K2, K1.

Row 2 (RS)

Small: K1, P4, 12 sts in double cable (row 2), RT, 12 sts in chain and double cable (row 2), RT, 12 sts in double cable, RT, 12 sts in chain and double cable, RT, P1, LT, 12 sts in chain and double cable, LT, 12 sts in double cable, LT, 12 sts in chain and double cable, LT, 12 sts in double cable, LT, P4, K1.

Medium: K1, P5, RT, K1, 12 sts in double cable (row 2), K1, RT, K1, 12 sts in chain and double cable (row 2), K1, RT, K1, 12 sts in double cable, K1, RT, K1, 12 sts in chain and double cable, K1, RT, P1, LT, K1, 12 sts in chain and double cable, K1, LT, K1, 12 sts in double cable, K1, LT, K1, 12 sts in chain and double cable, K1, LT, K1, 12 sts in double cable, K1, LT, P5, K1.

Large: K1, P8, RT, 12 sts in chain and double cable (row 2), RT, 12 sts in double cable (row 2), RT, 12 sts in chain and double cable, RT, 12 sts in double cable, RT, 12 sts in chain and double cable, RT, P1, LT, 12 sts in chain and double cable, LT, 12 sts in double cable, LT, 12 sts in chain and double cable, LT, 12 sts in double cable, LT, 12 sts in chain and double cable, LT, P8, K1.

Extra Large: K1, P2, RT, K1, 12 sts in chain and double cable (row 2), K1, RT, K1, 12 sts in double cable (row 2), K1, RT, K1, 12 sts in chain and double cable, K1, RT, K1, 12 sts in double cable, K1, RT, P2, LT, K1, 12 sts in chain and double cable, K1, LT, K1, 12 sts in double cable, K1, LT, K1, 12 sts in chain and double cable, K1, LT, K1, 12 sts in double cable, K1, LT, P2, K1.

Cont in main patt as est until 113 (117, 121, 127) rows have been worked. Work will measure approx 15 (15½, 16, 16½)" from beg.

Shape armholes: BO 4 (6, 6, 7) sts at beg of next 2 rows. Dec 1 st, then BO 2 (2, 3, 4) sts at beg of next 2 rows. Dec 1 st at each edge EOR 0 (0, 3, 3) times—113 (127, 137, 142) sts.

Cont even in patt as est until armhole measures 7½ (8, 8½, 9)", approx through row 180 (189, 197, 208).

Shape shoulders: BO 10 (11, 12, 13) sts at beg of next 2 rows. Dec 1 st, then BO 10 (11, 12, 13) sts at beg of next 2 rows. Dec 1 st, then BO 11 (13, 14, 14) sts at beg of next 2 rows. BO rem 47 (53, 57, 58) sts for neck edge.

fronts

With separate balls of yarn and size 4 needles, cable CO 64 (73, 82, 91) sts for each side of front. Work rows 1–27 as for back.

Change to larger needles and est main patt as follows.

Row 1 (WS)

Right front: K1, K4 (5, 8, 7), P0 (0, 2, 2), K0 (0, 0, 1), 12 sts in chain and double cable (row 1) 0 (0, 1, 1) times K0 (0, 0, 1), P2, K0 (1, 0, 1), 12 sts in double cable (row 1), K0 (1, 0, 1), P2, K0 (1, 0, 1), 12 sts in chain and double cable (row 1), K0 (1, 0, 1), P2, K0 (1, 0, 1), 12 sts in double cable, K0 (1, 0, 1), P2, K0 (1, 0, 1), 12 sts in chain and double cable, K0 (1, 0, 1), P2, K1.

Left front: K1, P2, K0 (1, 0, 1), 12 sts in chain and double cable, K0 (1, 0, 1), P2, K0 (1, 0, 1), 12 sts in double cable, K0 (1, 0, 1), P2, K0 (1, 0, 1), 12 sts in chain and double cable, K0 (1, 0, 1), P2, K0 (1, 0, 1), 12 sts in double cable, K0 (1, 0, 1), P2, K0 (0, 0, 1), 12 sts in chain and double cable 0 (0, 1, 1) times, K0 (0, 0, 1), P0 (0, 2, 2), K4 (5, 8, 7), K1.

Row 2

Left front: K1, P4 (5, 8, 7), RT 0 (0, 1, 1), P0 (0, 0, 1), 12 sts in chain and double cable (row 2) 0 (0, 1, 1) times, P0 (0, 0, 1), RT, P0 (1, 0, 1), 12 sts in double cable (row 2), P0 (1, 0, 1), RT, P0 (1, 0, 1), 12 sts in chain and double cable, P0 (1, 0, 1), RT, P0 (1, 0, 1) 12 sts in double cable, P0 (1, 0, 1), RT, P0 (1, 0, 1), 12 sts in chain and double cable, P0 (1, 0, 1), RT, K1.

Right front: K1, LT, P0 (1, 0, 1), 12 sts in chain and double cable, P0 (1, 0, 1), LT, P0 (1, 0, 1), 12 sts in double cable, P0 (1, 0, 1), LT, P0 (1, 0, 1), 12 sts in chain and double cable, P0 (1, 0, 1), LT, P0 (1, 0, 1), 12 sts in double cable, P0 (1, 0, 1), LT, P0 (0, 0, 1), 12 sts in chain and double cable 0 (0, 1, 1) times, P0 (0, 0, 1), LT 0 (0, 1, 1), P4 (5, 8, 7), K1.

Cont in main patt as est until same length as back to armhole.

Shape armholes: Work as for back—57 (64, 69, 76) sts. Cont in patt until work measures 21 (22, 23, 24)" from beg.

Shape neck and shoulders: BO 6 (7, 7, 7) sts pw on left front neck edge. BO 6 (7, 7, 7) sts kw on right front neck edge. Dec 1 st using P2tog tbl, then

BO 3 (4, 5, 5) sts pw on left front neck edge. Dec 1 st using ssk, then BO 3 (4, 5, 5) sts kw on right front neck edge. Cont to work decs as est for each neck edge: Dec 1 st, then BO 2 (2, 3, 4) sts. [Dec 1 st, then BO 2 (2, 2, 4) sts] twice for each side. Dec 1 st, then BO 1 (2, 2, 2) st. Dec 1 st, then BO 1 st. Dec 1 st and AT SAME TIME beg shoulder shaping at outer edge as for back.

sleeves

With separate balls of yarn and size 4 needles, cable CO 55 (64, 73, 82) sts for each sleeve. Work rows 1–26 as for back.

Row 27 (RS): Knit and inc 8 (7, 4, 2) sts evenly paced using M1 kw—63 (71, 77, 84) sts.

Shape sleeves:

Change to larger needles and est main patt as follows.

Row 1 (WS): K1, K0 (0, 7, 6), P2, K0 (1, 0, 1), 12 sts in double cable (row 1), K0 (1, 0, 1), P2, K0 (1, 0, 1), 12 sts in chain and double cable (row 1), K0 (1, 0, 1), P2, K1 (1, 1, 2), P2, K0 (1, 0, 1), 12 sts in chain and double cable, K0 (1, 0, 1), P2, K0 (1, 0, 1), 12 sts in double cable, K0 (1, 0, 1), P2, K0 (0, 7, 6), K1.

Row 2: K1, P0 (0, 7, 6), RT, P0 (1, 0, 1), 12 sts in double cable (row 2), P0 (1, 0, 1), RT, P0 (1, 0, 1), 12 sts in chain and double cable (row 2), P0 (1, 0, 1), RT, P1 (1, 1, 2), LT, P0 (1, 0, 1), 12 sts in chain and double cable, P0 (1, 0, 1), LT, P0 (1, 0, 1), 12 sts in double cable, P0 (1, 0, 1), LT, P0 (0, 7, 6), K1.

Cont in est patt, inc 1 st at each edge inside selvage sts beg row 8 and work this inc 14 (14, 15, 15) more times every 8 rows for a total of 93 (101, 109, 116) sts.

Work even until sleeve measures 16½ (17, 17½, 17½)", approx row 125 (131, 135, 135).

Shape caps: BO 4 (6, 6, 7) sts at beg of next 2 rows. Dec 1 st, then BO 2 (2, 3, 4) sts at beg of next 2 rows. Dec 1 st at beg of next 22 (26, 30, 32) rows. Dec 1 st at each edge of next 11 rows. Dec 1 st, then BO 2 sts at beg of next 2 rows. Dec 1 st, then BO 3 sts at beg of next 2 rows. BO rem 21 (21, 23, 24) sts.

finishing

Meticulously block pieces to measurements.

Sew shoulder seams using invisible horizontal seaming, referring to "Joining Textured Shoulders" on page 12.

Left front button band: With size 4 needles and RS of work facing you, PU from left to right 140 (150, 152, 162) sts.

Row 1 (RS): K1 (0, 1, 0), *K2, P2, rep from * to last 3 (2, 3, 2) sts, K3 (2, 3, 2).

Row 2: K1 (0, 1, 0), *P2, K2, rep from * to last 3 (2, 3, 2) sts, P2 (1, 2, 1), K1.

Rows 3–6: Rep rows 1 and 2.

Row 7: BO all sts in patt.

Right front buttonhole band: Work as for button band through row 2.

Row 3: Work 4 (3, 4, 3) sts in patt, *turn and work sts in patt (row 4), turn and work sts in patt (row 5). Leaving a tail, cut yarn. Attach yarn to next st, work 12 sts in patt; rep from * 10 (12, 12, 13) times, work last buttonhole, end work with 4 (3, 4, 3) sts in patt. Note that this type of buttonhole looks best when worked between 2 purl sts.

Row 6: Work in patt across row, joining all sections. Pick up cut strand of yarn from buttonhole edge and as you purl that st to connect edges, use 2 strands of yarn (yarn from ball and cut strand) to secure edge for this st and the next st only.

Row 7: BO all sts in patt.

Use the yarn tails near the buttonholes to reinforce each buttonhole using buttonhole st (see page 11).

Sew sleeves into armholes using invisible vertical to horizontal seaming.

Sew side seams and underarm seams using invisible vertical on reverse St st seaming.

Collar: With size 4 needles, cable CO 127 (145, 163, 172) sts and work rows 1–26 as for back.

Transfer these sts to a long circular needle or a piece of waste yarn and block to 2½" x 19 (21½, 24, 25½)". Transfer sts back to needle and work last row as K1, P7, P3tog, *P6, P3tog, rep from * to last 8 sts, P7, K1—101 (115, 129, 136) sts.

Leave these sts on needle.

With size 3 circular needle, PU 30 (35, 38, 40) sts at left front, 41 (45, 53, 56) sts at back of neck, and 30 (35, 38, 40) sts at right front—101 (115, 129, 136) sts. Work 2 rows as follows to create a stand for your collar.

Row 1: (RS) K1 (1, 1, 0), *P1, K1, rep from *.

Row 2: K1 (1, 1, 0), *K1, P1, rep from * to last 2 sts, K2.

Place RS of collar against WS of garment, and with an extra size 3 needle, work 3-needle BO to attach collar.

Grosgrain ribbon: By hand, whipstitch grosgrain ribbon in place to face the inside of the collar. Position the ribbon to cover the ridge created by picking up neck stitches on one long edge of ribbon. Position other long edge to meet the knot edge of the

knotted cable. At the neck edge, fold the raw edge of the ribbon under slightly (between ⅛" and ¼") and press in place, then fold once more and press again to create a firmer facing edge at neck edge.

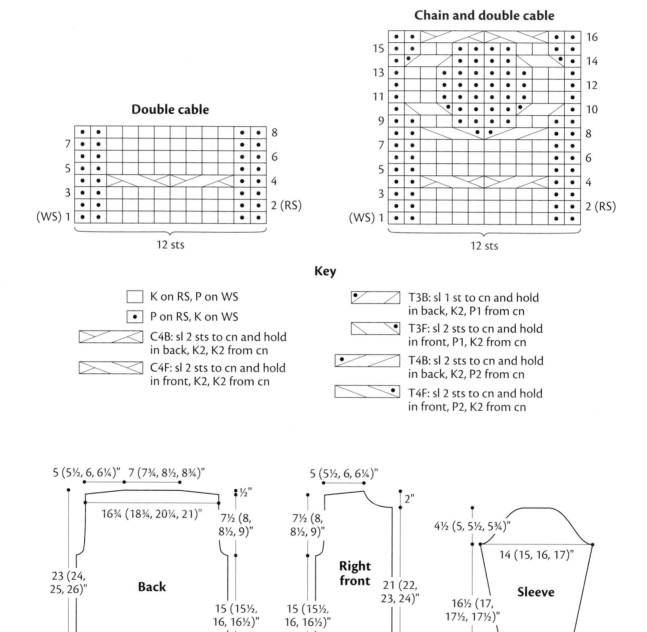

CHAIN AND DOUBLE CABLE CARDIGAN AND SOCKS

SOCK INSTRUCTIONS

Leg

Using size 4 dpns, somewhat loosely cable CO 63 (72) sts.

Rnd 1: *K2, P2, K2, P3; rep from *, dividing sts into 18-27-18 (18-36-18) over 3 dpns and join into rnd, being careful not to twist work. Work another 7 rnds as est.

Rnd 9: *Sl 2 sts to cn and hold at back, sl 2 sts to another cn and hold at front, P2tog, K2 from cn at front, P2tog from cn at back, P3; rep from * —14-21-14 (14-28-14) per dpn and 49 (56) sts total.

Rnds 10 and 11: P1, *K2, P5; rep from * to last 6 sts, K2, P4.

Rnd 12: *Sl 1 st to cn and hold at back, sl 2 sts to another cn and hold at front, K1f&b in next st, P2 from cn at front, K1f&b in st on cn at back, P3; rep from * around—63 (72) sts.

Rnds 13–22: *K2, P2, K2, P3; rep from * around.

Rnds 23–25: Rep rnds 9–11.

Rnd 26: *Sl 1 st to cn and hold at back, sl 2 sts to another cn and hold at front, K1f&b in next st, P2 from cn at front, K1f&b in st on cn at back, P2tog, P1; rep from * around—14-28-14 (16-32-16) sts per dpn and 56 (64) sts total.

Rnd 27: *K2, P2; rep from * around.

Cont in ribbing until leg measures 6½" or desired length to top of heel.

heel flap

Work 14 (16) sts in est ribbing patt, turn work and P28 (32) sts on 1 needle. Place rem 28 (32) sts on spare needle or holder. Work heel flap as follows.

Row 1 (RS): *Sl 1 pw wyib, K1; rep from *.

Row 2: Sl 1 pw wyif, purl to end.

Rep rows 1 and 2 until heel flap measures 2½", ending with WS row.

turn heel

Work short rows as follows:

Row 1 (RS): Sl 1, K15 (17), ssk, K1, turn work.

Row 2: Sl 1 pw, P5, P2tog, P1, turn work.

Row 3: Sl 1 pw, knit to 1 st before gap made on previous row, ssk (1 st from each side of gap), K1, turn work.

Row 4: Sl 1 pw, purl to 1 st before gap made on previous row, P2tog (1 st from each side of gap), P1, turn work.

Rep rows 3 and 4 until all heel sts have been worked, ending with WS row. Note that last rep of row 3 will end with ssk and last rep of row 4 will end with P2tog—16 (18) sts.

gusset

Rnd 1: With 1 dpn, knit across all heel sts, then PU 15 (17) sts along selvage edge of heel flap. With another dpn, knit across 28 (32) instep sts. With another dpn, PU 15 (17) sts along other side of heel flap and knit across the first 8 (9) heel sts from the first needle again—74 (84) sts total and 23-28-23 (26-32-26) sts distributed over 3 needles with rnd now beg at center-back heel again.

Rnd 2: On first needle, knit to last 3 sts, K2tog, K1; on second needle, knit across all instep sts; on third needle, K1, ssk, knit to end—2 gusset sts decreased.

Rnd 3: Knit.

Rep rnds 2 and 3 until 56 (64) sts total rem, 14-28-14 (16-32-16) sts distributed over 3 needles.

foot

Work even until foot measures 6½" from center back of heel or 2½" less than desired total length for foot; the measurement of the bottom of your foot. Length given above works for shoe size 6–7. Work as needed for additional length.

toe

Rnd 1: On first needle, knit to last 3 sts, K2tog, K1; on second needle, K1, ssk, work to last 3 sts, K2tog, K1; on third needle, K1, ssk, knit to end—4 sts decreased.

Rnd 2: Knit.

Rep rnds 1 and 2 until 16 (20) total sts rem, ending with rnd 1. Knit sts from first needle onto third needle—8 (10) sts each on 2 needles.

finishing

Cut yarn, leaving 18" tail, and use kitchener st to graft toe sts tog. Weave in loose ends. Block if desired or wear to block.

Rep for other sock.

REFERENCE

ABBREVIATIONS AND GLOSSARY

approx	approximately
beg	begin(ning)
BO	bind off
cn	cable needle(s)
CO	cast on
cont	continue(ing)(s)
dec	decrease(ing)(s)
dpn(s)	double-pointed needle(s)
EOR	every other row
est	established
g	gram(s)
inc	increase(ing)(s)
K	knit
K1f&b	knit into front and back of same stitch—1 stitch increased
K2tog	knit 2 stitches together—1 stitch decreased
kw	knitwise
M1 kw	make 1 stitch knitwise—1 stitch increased. (See page 13.)
M1 pw	make 1 stitch purlwise—1 stitch increased. (See page 13.)
m	meter(s)
oz	ounce(s)
P	purl
P1f&b	purl into front and back of same stitch—1 stitch increased

P2tog	purl 2 stitches together—1 stitch decreased
P3tog	purl 3 stitches together—2 stitches decreased
patt(s)	pattern(s)
psso	pass slipped stitch over
PU	pick up and knit
pw	purlwise
rem	remain(ing)
rep(s)	repeat(s)
rnd(s)	round(s)
RS	right side
sk	skip
sl	slip
sl 1	slip 1 stitch purlwise unless otherwise intrructed
ssk	slip, slip, knit—1 stitch decreased. (See page 76.)
ssp	slip, slip, purl—1 stitch decreased. (See page 76.)
st(s)	stitch(es)
St st(s)	stockinette stitch(es) (knit on right side, purl on wrong side)
tbl	through back loop(s)
tog	together
wyib	with yarn in back
wyif	with yarn in front
WS	wrong side
yd(s)	yard(s)
YO(s)	yarn over(s)

BLOCKING

Blocking is a step of finishing that should not be overlooked and is the key to a garment's final appearance. Meticulous blocking enhances your knitting and makes your finished garment more beautiful. It involves steaming your garment to even out stitching lines and yarn fibers, since many stitches or patterns require opening up and evening out. This is especially true of sweaters with lots of texture, whether there are lacy, open stitches or multiple cables.

I like to block on the floor. I use a very thick towel and put it down on top of carpet. If you can find a towel that has a pattern on it resembling graph paper, or even one with larger squares or lines, it can be a helpful guideline. Blocking boards work well and are usually available at your local yarn shop.

Begin by pinning your garment pieces to the towel or board to match the measurements shown in the schematic for each piece. Lay the work down flat and smooth. Straighten and open the stitches as you pin down the edges; use lots of pins. Pin every ¼" to ½", depending on the pattern. Nice edges make nice seams. I like to pin both the back and front pieces at the same time and both sleeves at the same time to ensure accurate measurements and symmetry. Once you think you have the pieces pinned and shaped to perfection, walk away and take a break so that you can come back to the project later with a fresh eye for that last check. This is important, and I almost always notice some tiny detail in this last step before steaming.

To steam, simply fill an iron with water and preheat it. Cover the work to be blocked with a clean linen tea towel. With a spray bottle of water, dampen the tea towel. Then hold the iron lightly on the damp towel without pressure, and steam iron each area of the work evenly. Be sure not to miss edges. If you use long pins with a bead-type round head for pinning, you will feel where the edges are. I leave each piece pinned down overnight for thorough drying.

BACKWARD LOOP CAST ON

This is a looser cast on which creates an edge that makes it easy to pick up stitches. Loops can be formed over the index finger or thumb and slanted to the left.

Backward loop cast on

CABLE CAST ON

Cable cast on is my preferred way to cast on because it produces a nice edge.

Insert needle between first 2 stitches. Wrap yarn around the right needle and pull through to make a stitch.

Place new stitch on the left needle.

KNIT CAST ON

I use the knit cast on to add stitches to the neck on the Moss and Feather Faggot Shell on page 36. The only difference between the knit cast on and the cable cast on is that you insert the right-hand needle into the first stitch instead of between two stitches.

Knit into the first stitch on the left needle. Do not drop the stitch off.

Place the new stitch on the left needle.

DECREASES

In working single decreases, I use K2tog tbl or ssk (see page 76) at the beginning of the row and K2tog at the end of the row on right-side rows, regardless of stitch patterns. On a wrong-side row, I use P2tog tbl or ssp (see page 76) at the beginning of the row and P2tog at the end of the row so that the bumps created by the purl stitches are on the wrong side of the knitting. Remember that these decreased stitches will end up in a seam. I prefer the seam edge to be as smooth as possible.

In working decreases on curved or tapered edges—such as shaping armholes, sleeve caps or shoulders, and certain types of necklines—my method is slightly different for binding off the subsequent rows after the initial row. I use a normal bind off for the initial bind-off row to define the edge. Then for all following rows with stitches to be bound off, I choose to work the first two stitches together (as in K2tog tbl or P2tog tbl) and pass that over the next stitch before continuing to bind off the instructed number of stitches. Working the first two stitches together produces a smoother curved edge and less of a bump or step than binding off the first stitch in the normal manner. I believe this promotes better seaming and a smoother neckline.

Here's an example of standard directions for armhole shaping:

BO 3 sts at beg of next 2 rows.

BO 2 sts at beg of next 2 rows.

BO 1 st at beg of next 2 rows.

In this book, the previous directions for armhole shaping are written as follows.

BO 3 sts at beg of next 2 rows.

Dec 1 st, then BO 1 st at beg of next 2 rows.

Dec 1 st at beg of next 2 rows.

As you can see, the first set of bind offs (BO 3) are the same for each set of directions. I would bind off three stitches knitwise, assuming that this is a right-side row, and then bind off three stitches purlwise, assuming that this is a wrong-side row. The difference between the standard method and my method occurs at the beginning of the next two rows. On a right-side row, I work K2tog tbl or ssk (one stitch is gone), K1 and pass the K2tog tbl or ssk stitch over the K1 (two stitches are gone). On a wrong-side row, I work P2tog tbl or ssp, P1, and pass the P2tog tbl or ssp stitch over the P1. For the final two rows, I would simply K2tog tbl or P2tog tbl.

Slip, slip, knit (ssk). Slip one stitch as if to knit, slip one stitch as if to knit, insert the left needle into front of the two stitches, knit the two stitches together.

Slip, slip, purl (ssp). Slip one stitch as if to knit, slip one stitch as if to knit, return the two stitches back to left needle, purl two stitches together through the back loops.

KITCHENER STITCH

To work the kitchener stitch to close the toe stitches on a sock, you must have the same number of stitches on each needle. Cut the yarn, leaving an 18" tail, and thread through a tapestry needle. Hold the needles parallel to each other and work from right to left with the yarn coming from the back needle.

Insert the tapestry needle in the front stitch as if to purl and leave the stitch on the needle. Insert the tapestry needle in the first stitch on the back needle as if to knit and leave the stitch on the needle. *Now insert the tapestry needle in the first stitch on the front needle as if to knit and slip it off. Insert the tapestry needle in the next stitch on the front needle as if to purl, and leave the stitch on the needle. Insert the tapestry needle in the front stitch on the back needle as if to purl and slip it off. Insert the tapestry needle in the next stitch on the back needle as if to knit and leave the stitch on the needle. Repeat from * until one stitch remains. Pull the end through the last stitch and weave the end inside of the toe.

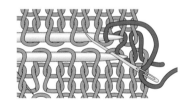

SEAMING

Different seaming techniques are appropriate for different areas of a garment. They make the difference in a professional-looking garment. Work all seaming techniques with the right side of the work facing you, and secure the tail at the end of the seam. Weave the tail into the wrong side of the garment vertically using a tapestry needle or crochet hook. If you weave a tail in horizontally, you will create a ridge.

Beginning seaming. The way to begin seaming is with a figure eight. Use a long tail (about 18") from a cast-on row to thread your tapestry needle. With the right sides of pieces to be seamed facing you, insert the tapestry needle from back to front into the corner stitch of the work without the tail. You will then make a figure eight with the tail, which might be more accurately described as the infinity sign, since the eight is lying on its side. Insert the needle from back to front into the stitch with the cast-on tail. Gently tighten or secure to close the beginning of the seam.

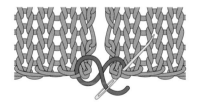

Invisible horizontal for shoulders. Line up the bound-off edges stitch for stitch. Insert the tapestry needle under a stitch inside the bound-off edge of one side and under the corresponding stitch on the other side. Close the edge by pulling the yarn snugly enough to hide the bound-off edges and continue to the next stitch. Note that you must have the same number of stitches on each piece to be joined.

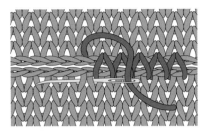

Invisible vertical to horizontal for setting in sleeves. Insert the tapestry needle under a stitch inside the bound-off edge of the vertical piece. Now insert the tapestry needle under one or two horizontal bars (as appropriate: one bar is appropriate when the length of the vertical and horizontal piece is identical, and two bars are appropriate when easing in fullness) between the first and second stitches of the horizontal piece. Continue in this manner.

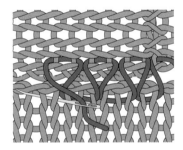

Invisible vertical on stockinette stitch for side and underarm seams. This technique joins edges row by row, hides selvage stitches, and makes your knitting appear continuous. Insert the tapestry needle under the horizontal bar between the first and second stitches. Insert the needle into the corresponding bar on the other

piece. Secure the seam gently yet firmly, and continue alternating from side to side.

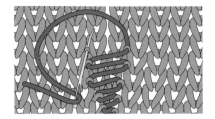

Invisible vertical on reverse stockinette stitch for side and underarm seams. Instead of working into the horizontal strand between the stitches, work into the stitch itself. Insert the tapestry needle into the top loop of the stitch inside the edge on one side and then into the bottom loop of the corresponding stitch on the other side. Secure the seam gently yet firmly and continue alternating side to side.

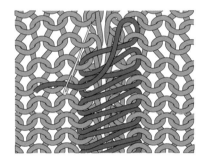

WHIPSTITCH

With threaded tapestry needle and working from right to left, make slanted stitches about 1/8" to 1/4" deep and 1/8" to 1/4" apart (depending on the weight of the knitted fabric; make them closer for finer knits). Make

stitches one at a time and pull the yarn through snugly without pulling the knitting too tight.

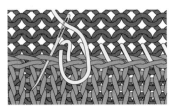

SWATCHING

Swatching is the actual knitting of a stitch pattern you plan to use in a knit garment. Swatches are most often knit in a 4" by 4" square. Swatching is an essential part of creating the sweater you want. Not only does it confirm gauge, but it tells you if the yarn you have chosen will give you the look you want for your garment, particularly in terms of weight and drape. Pin your swatch down as if to block it when calculating gauge. Count your stitches and rows per inch over several inches.

THREE-NEEDLE BIND OFF (3-NEEDLE BO)

The three-needle bind off produces a lovely seam. To work, place right sides together with the back stitches on one needle and the front stitches on another. Using a third needle of the same size, *knit two stitches together (one from the front needle and one from the back needle)*; repeat from * to * once and pass the first stitch over the second stitch. Repeat this until all stitches are bound off, and secure edge.

$\mathcal{U}$seful INFORMATION

STANDARD YARN-WEIGHT SYSTEM

Yarn-Weight Symbol and Category Name	0 Lace	1 Super Fine	2 Fine	3 Light	4 Medium	5 Bulky	6 Super Bulky
Types of Yarn in Category	Fingering 10-count crochet thread	Sock, Fingering, Baby	Sport, Baby	DK, Light Worsted	Worsted, Afghan, Aran	Chunky, Craft, Rug	Bulky, Roving
Knit Gauge Range* in Stockinette Stitch to 4"	33 to 40** sts	27 to 32 sts	23 to 26 sts	21 to 24 sts	16 to 20 sts	12 to 15 sts	6 to 11 sts
Recommended Needle in Metric Size Range	1.5 to 2.25 mm	2.25 to 3.25 mm	3.25 to 3.75 mm	3.75 to 4.5 mm	4.5 to 5.5 mm	5.5 to 8 mm	8 mm and larger
Recommended Needle in U.S. Size Range	000 to 1	1 to 3	3 to 5	5 to 7	7 to 9	9 to 11	11 and larger

*These are guidelines only. The above reflect the most commonly used gauges and needle or hook sizes for specific yarn categories.

**Lace-weight yarns are usually knit or crocheted on larger needles and hooks to create lacy, openwork patterns. Accordingly, a gauge range is difficult to determine. Always follow the gauge stated in your pattern.

SKILL LEVEL

■□□□ **Beginner.** Projects for first-time knitters using basic knit and purl stitches. Minimal shaping.

■■□□ **Easy.** Projects using basic stitches, repetitive stitch patterns, and simple color changes. Simple shaping and finishing.

■■■□ **Intermediate.** Projects using a variety of stitches, such as basic cables and lace, simple intarsia, and techniques for double-pointed needles and knitting in the round. Mid-level shaping.

■■■■ **Experienced.** Projects using advanced techniques and stitches, such as short rows, Fair Isle, intricate intarsia, cables, lace patterns, and numerous color changes.

METRIC CONVERSIONS

m	=	yds	x	0.9144
yds	=	m	x	1.0936
g	=	oz	x	28.35
oz	=	g	x	0.0352

RESOURCES

Contact the following companies to find shops that carry the yarn in this book.

Brown Sheep Company, Inc.

www.brownsheep.com

Cotton Fine

Nature Spun Sportweight

Lamb's Pride Worsted

Elann.com

www.elann.com

Endless Summer Collection Sonata

Kertzer

www.kertzer.com

Butterfly Super 10

Louet Sales

www.louet.com

Gems Worsted Weight

Gems Topaz

Misti International, Inc.

www.mistialpaca.com

Misti Alpaca

Tahki Imports, Ltd.

www.tahkistacycharles.com

Cotton Classic

KNITTING and CROCHET TITLES

ACCESSORIES

Crocheted Pursenalities

Crocheted Socks!

Kitty Knits

Pursenalities

Pursenality Plus

Stitch Style: Mittens

BABIES, CHILDREN & TOYS

Berets, Beanies, and Booties

Crochet for Tots

Gigi Knits…and Purls—*NEW!*

Knitting with Gigi

Too Cute!

CROCHET

365 Crochet Stitches a Year:
  Perpetual Calendar

Amigurumi World

A to Z of Crochet

First Crochet

KNITTING

200 Knitted Blocks

365 Knitting Stitches a Year:
  Perpetual Calendar

A to Z of Knitting

Cable Confidence—*NEW!*

Casual, Elegant Knits—*NEW!*

Chic Knits

Fair Isle Sweaters Simplified

First Knits

Handknit Skirts

Handknit Style II

Knit One, Stripe Too

The Knitter's Book of
  Finishing Techniques

Knitting Beyond the Basics

Modern Classics

Ocean Breezes

Romantic Style

Silk Knits

Simple Gifts for Dog Lovers

Skein for Skein—*NEW!*

Special Little Knits from
  Just One Skein

Stripes, Stripes, Stripes

Top Down Sweaters

Wrapped in Comfort

The Yarn Stash Workbook

LITTLE BOX SERIES

The Little Box of Crochet for
  Baby

The Little Box of Crocheted Gifts

The Little Box of
  Crocheted Scarves

The Little Box of
  Crocheted Throws

The Little Box of Knits for Baby

The Little Box of Knitted Gifts

The Little Box of Knitted Throws

The Little Box of Socks

SOCK KNITTING

Knitting Circles around Socks

More Sensational Knitted Socks

Sensational Knitted Socks

Stitch Style: Socks

Martingale ®
& C O M P A N Y

America's Best-Loved Craft & Hobby Books ®
America's Best-Loved Knitting Books ®

Our books are available at bookstores and your favorite craft, fabric, and yarn retailers. If you don't see the title you're looking for, visit us at **www.martingale-pub.com** or contact us at:

1-800-426-3126

International: 1-425-483-3313

Fax: 1-425-486-7596 • **Email:** info@martingale-pub.com